"Taking their school-based approach ar[...] the authors enlarge the audience who c[...] vention program. The program is well-[...] and systematic strategies that are both [...] on established principles of learning, the program [...] s parents in how to teach, shape, and practice a step-by-step method for youth to overcome the fear of speaking. A welcomed addition to the literature that strives to reduce anxiety in youth, I encourage parents to read and apply the program."

—*Philip C. Kendall, Ph.D., ABPP, Laura H. Carnell Professor of Psychology and director of the Child and Adolescent Anxiety Disorders Clinic at Temple University*

"Finally, parents of children who suffer from selective mutism have a comprehensive, well-written resource to help them deal with this challenging problem. This book provides a thorough description of the disorder as well as a detailed, practical, step-by-step program for helping the child overcome selective mutism once and for all. If someone you care about suffers from selective mutism, this book is a must! It is also a great resource for teachers and for professionals who treat selective mutism."

—*Martin M. Antony, Ph.D., ABPP, director of the Anxiety Treatment and Research Centre at St. Joseph's Healthcare and professor in the Department of Psychiatry and Behavioural Neurosciences at McMaster University, Hamilton, ON*

"This is, without exception, the best book for parents on the topic of selective mutism I have had the pleasure to read. Loaded with information on the nature and causes of this childhood condition and filled with practical advice on how to cope with and effectively treat it, this book provides parents with a highly useful, trustworthy, science-based program for the child with selective mutism. Few if any professionals have more clinical experience with such children and the treatment of their condition than do McHolm and Cunningham. My congratulations both to the authors for putting together such a finely crafted book and to you, the reader, for having the good sense to buy it."

—*Russell A. Barkley, Ph.D., research professor of psychiatry at the State University of New York Upstate Medical School in Syracuse, NY*

"Silence, indeed, is not always golden. *Helping Your Child with Selective Mutism* is a must-read for parents, educators, clinicians, and developmental researchers. McHolm and her colleagues have provided a scholarly, lucid, and practical account of how to understand and manage the child with selective mutism. The authors' step-by-step program will help even the most silent child."

—*Louis A. Schmidt, Ph.D., associate professor of psychology and director of the Child Emotion Laboratory at McMaster University in Hamilton, ON*

"Finally! A well-informed perspective on an often undiagnosed, mismanaged, and misunderstood childhood anxiety disorder. The practical insights of Drs. McHolm and Cunningham and Ms. Vanier are necessary reading for parents and teachers alike. These are real strategies that can be easily incorporated into a classroom setting! *Helping Your Child with Selective Mutism* is a necessary addition to the bookshelves of parents and teachers everywhere!"

—*Lin Gorenkoff, parent of a child formerly with selective mutism, and facilitator and founder of the Selectively Silent Child Support Group and Web site, www.designandcopy.ca/silentchild*

"The practical strategies in this book—focusing on progress rather than failure—were instrumental in helping our child overcome selective mutism. Our son's anxiety toward speaking at school has disappeared entirely. He is now considerably more self-confident and sociable, speaking freely to his teachers and friends. I would highly recommend this approach to selective mutism to any family facing the same challenge."

—*Anthony Sraka, school teacher in Oakville, ON, Canada, and father of a child formerly with selective mutism*

Helping Your Child *with* Selective Mutism

PRACTICAL STEPS
TO OVERCOME A
FEAR *of* SPEAKING

ANGELA E. M^cHOLM, PH.D.
CHARLES E. CUNNINGHAM, PH.D.
MELANIE K. VANIER, MA

New Harbinger Publications, Inc.

Distributed in Canada by Raincoast Books

Copyright © 2005 by Angela E. McHolm, Charles E. Cunningham,
and Melanie K. Vanier
New Harbinger Publications, Inc.
5674 Shattuck Avenue
Oakland, CA 94609

Cover design by Amy Shoup; Cover image: Creatas/PhotoAlto;
Acquired by Tesilya Hanauer; Edited by Karen O'Donnell Stein;
Text design by Tracy Marie Carlson

Library of Congress Cataloging-in-Publication Data

McHolm, Angela E.
  Helping your child with selective mutism : practical steps to overcome a fear of speaking / Angela E. McHolm, Charles E. Cunningham, and Melanie K. Vanier.
     p. cm.
  Includes bibliographical references.
  ISBN-10: 1-57224-416-X
  ISBN-13: 978-1-57224-416-0
  1. Mutism, Elective—Popular works. I. Cunningham, Charles E. II. Vanier, Melanie K. III. Title.
  RJ506.M87M34 2005
  616.92'84—dc22

                              2005014370

New Harbinger Publications' website address: www.newharbinger.com

11   10   09
10   9   8   7   6

FSC
Mixed Sources
Product group from well-managed
forests and other controlled sources
Cert no. SW-COC-002283
www.fsc.org
© 1996 Forest Stewardship Council

Contents

Foreword

Fifteen years ago when I was a novice lecturer in psychology, I supervised the clinical work of a student who had been asked to see a young child who was selectively mute. The child, let's call him Peter, was seven years old and had never spoken to anyone at school, despite the fact that his parents said that they couldn't stop him from talking at home. Like any good therapist, I told the student to search the scientific literature to find the best tested and most thoroughly supported treatments. When she returned to tell me that she could not find a single large, properly conducted study, I was shocked. We spoke to school personnel and a variety of mental health professionals and were given an incredible array of suggestions. In the end, we did the best we could, based on standard psychological principles, and Peter gradually broadened his circle of accepted confidants.

Over the past fifteen years, very little has changed. We do know a little more about selective mutism, and some descriptive research is beginning to appear. But there is still relatively little solid research into the best treatment techniques and, most frighteningly, the folklore and false information surrounding this problem are still widespread. That is one reason that this book is so important. A few months ago I was interviewed on a local television program about selective mutism. The program had filmed a young girl in grade one who did not speak to her teachers or to the other children in class. The school had been considering sending her to a special school for developmentally delayed children. I spoke on the program about the links between selective mutism and anxiety, and about how these children could be seen as similar to extremely shy children. I also talked about the fact that there was no link between selective mutism and low intelligence. After the program aired, I received many calls from parents who were angry, relieved, and grateful. They were angry because of the tremendous runaround that many of them had received from the educational and health systems. Many had been told that their child had a developmental delay such as autism, while others had been told that their child was simply being naughty or willful and loved the attention that she or he received by not speaking. Many were also told that there was nothing that could be done, that it was "just a phase," and that their child would soon get sick of not speaking or grow out of it. And they were relieved and grateful because finally someone was giving them information that made sense. Parents of selectively mute children know that their child is not delayed or naughty, but they do need to know that the problem is being studied and that there do exist some good programs to help.

Despite what many parents of selectively mute children have been told, selective mutism is a very real problem that can have devastating effects on a child's life and the lives of those closest to them. It can be one of the most confusing and frustrating of problems because parents know their child's spark and wit, only to be told by friends and teachers about a withdrawn, silent stranger. We also don't know the long-term effects of selective mutism. But we do know that extreme shyness can tremendously limit a child's life and that very shy and anxious children are at increased risk for a wide range of problems as they grow. That is why early help can be so important.

When Angela asked me to write the foreword to this book, I readily agreed. Because there is so little good information out there about the best ways to treat selective mutism, and information for parents is so scarce and confusing, this book fills an important gap. As a parent of a selectively mute child, it may be one of the most important books you ever read. The book is sensitively written and provides clear structure, information, and content. It is a book that provides parents with practical examples and detailed information, either so that they can help their own child or so that they know what a professional should be doing to help them and their child. Selective mutism is a type of anxiety problem, and the advances in the management of anxiety in children over the past ten years are of great help in the management of selective mutism. But selectively mute children do have their own patterns and quirks that need special strategies. The information in this book is based on the most up-to-date scientific information and describes methods of helping selectively mute children that are based on cutting-edge strategies. The team at McMaster Children's Hospital led by Angela, Charles, and Melanie has had years of experience studying and helping children with selective mutism and their families, and the authors have brought together all of their collective expertise and sensitivity in writing these pages. I know that this book will answer the wishes of many parents with selectively mute children and I will be pointing my own clients to it for many years.

—Ronald M. Rapee
Professor of Psychology and Director,
Macquarie University Anxiety Research Unit
Macquarie University, Sydney, Australia

Introduction

Although there are various explanations for the condition, selective mutism is most likely anxiety based. Selective mutism is thought to reflect a fear of being heard (or seen) speaking in certain situations leading a child to speak in some settings while not in others. Given the condition's basis in anxiety, strategies proven to be helpful in dealing with other forms of fear or anxiety are the main focus of this book. Regardless of the extent of your child's selective mutism, the strategies outlined in this book can be helpful if your child doesn't speak at times because of anxiety. What this book can't do is anticipate every unique example of selective mutism or provide every piece of information a parent would need to know to help. For this reason, we strongly recommend that you consult a professional on behalf of your child. The information and strategies you will learn about in this book can complement your work with a mental-health professional, medical professional, or other service provider.

IS SELECTIVE MUTISM A NEW CONDITION?

Despite the fact that the term *selective mutism* was adopted only recently in the scientific literature, scientists and mental-health professionals have been describing children who speak in some but not other situations for over a century. As far back as 1877, a German physician by the name of Clifton Kussmaul first described a disorder called *aphasia voluntaria*, in which people didn't speak in certain settings despite being fully capable of speech. Nearly sixty years later, in 1934, a Swiss psychiatrist named Moritz Tramer coined the term *elective mutism* to describe these children. Tramer's use of the adjective *elective* illustrated the belief dominant at the time that these children were choosing or electing not to speak. Experts in the field have since come to appreciate that a child's mutism may not be a matter of choice or free will. The current term, *selective mutism* (American Psychiatric Association 1994), is thought to more accurately reflect the condition, in which the child feels comfortable speaking only in select or particular situations.

ABOUT THE AUTHORS

Dr. Angela McHolm is a clinical psychologist who serves as the director of the Selective Mutism Service at McMaster Children's Hospital in Hamilton, Ontario, Canada. The Selective Mutism Service offers consultation and clinical services to families and professionals supporting a child with selective mutism. Dr. McHolm has been responsible for the development of a large-group workshop series for parents and professionals, a training program for professionals, and models of individual therapy suited to older children with selective mutism. In addition to providing clinical services and consultation, Dr. McHolm presents widely on the topic and is engaged in several research ventures with Dr. Charles Cunningham.

Dr. Charles Cunningham is the clinical director of the Community Education Service at McMaster Children's Hospital, a professor of psychiatry and behavioural neurosciences, and the Jack Laidlaw Chair in Patient-Centered Health Care in the Faculty of Health Sciences at McMaster University, Hamilton, Ontario, Canada. Dr. Cunningham has published and presented widely on various topics related to children's mental health. Within the field of selective mutism, Dr. Cunningham has approximately thirty years of clinical experience and has coauthored various publications on the subject. Most notably, the intervention approach described in this book is based on his program, which he laid out in his book *COPEing with Selective Mutism: A Collaborative School-Based Approach* (2001). The book you are reading represents a parent-geared extension of Dr. Cunningham's original guide, with important adaptations and additions for the interested parent.

Melanie Vanier, at the time of writing this book, worked as a clinician with the Selective Mutism Service at McMaster Children's Hospital. In addition to her clinical work with the program, Ms. Vanier collaborated on the development and writing of a manualized, large-group workshop series for parents and professionals and a training program for professionals. She was also participated in the evaluation of clinical services provided by the Selective Mutism Service. Ms. Vanier is near completion of a Ph.D. in child clinical psychology.

WHY WAS THIS BOOK WRITTEN?

Through our clinical work with children with selective mutism, we've been introduced to a highly committed group of parents who are motivated to learn more about selective mutism, the related issues to be faced, and how best to support their children. In an effort to direct parents toward helpful, high-quality readings on the subject, we've searched high and low for suitable resources. It's been our experience, however, that relatively few publications are available on the subject. Of what exists, very few resources are geared toward parents struggling to make sense of their child's limited speaking patterns, the impact of these patterns on their child's daily functioning, and the role parents can play in supporting their child with selective mutism. As a result, parents can be left feeling helpless, isolated, and questioning the validity of their concerns for their child. Parents of children with selective mutism are often heard making self-doubting remarks, such as "My family thinks he's just shy, so maybe I shouldn't worry" and "My family physician has told me that she will grow out of it." Have you uttered these kinds of comments? Have you wondered what you can do as a parent to find out more and how you can help?

HOW TO USE THIS BOOK

We hope that this book will provide you as a parent with valuable information about selective mutism, based on the available research and clinical experience of experts in the field. You'll be provided an overview of what is currently understood about the condition, what professional services may be helpful, and what general parenting issues might be relevant. Most important, you'll be introduced to a collaborative, school-based intervention program in which you can play a significant role. By making information and strategies available to you, the parent, we hope you'll learn that you can be actively involved in helping your child overcome selective mutism both in and outside of school.

As you read, you'll see that the book is organized in three sections to provide you with an overview of selective mutism, details of how to plan an effective intervention program, and information about how to maintain your child's progress. This step-by-step guide will describe specific strategies that you, and the professionals assisting you, can use to help your child work through her fear of speaking. In order to make sure you understand each strategy and how it would apply to your child's situation, you'll have the opportunity to work through exercises that allow you to think about your own child's situation and what might help. To keep track of your ideas as you work through the exercises, you'll need a notebook or journal to write down your thoughts and questions. If you don't already have a notebook you can use, you'll need to pick one up before moving on to chapter 1.

TWO EXAMPLES OF CHILDREN WITH SELECTIVE MUTISM

Let's begin our discussion of this condition by looking at two examples of children displaying typical signs of selective mutism. We believe these children would benefit from the strategies described in this book. Throughout the book, we will describe other children with selective mutism as a means to show you how the described techniques can be applied to real-life situations.

Sarah is a six-year-old student in a regular first-grade class. At the age of three, Sarah was assessed by a speech and language pathologist because she had trouble articulating her words. Sarah received short-term speech therapy and her mother now reports that her speech is fine. She describes Sarah as a chatterbox when she's at home and with immediate family. She also reports that Sarah will engage in polite conversation with adults in the community, like the grocery clerk or the crossing guard. Sarah's family has moved two times since she started school, and she has changed neighborhoods and schools with each move.

Sarah's current teacher says she is well liked in her class and is often invited into play by her peers. However, Sarah speaks to only one child in the class, a girl who was enrolled in the same day-care center three years ago. She speaks to her one friend at school in certain situations, such as when they are alone on the playground. She doesn't speak to her teacher at all and in fact has never spoken to any of the adults at her school.

Peter is an eleven-year-old sixth-grade student at a large inner-city school. Peter moved to this country approximately five years ago with his parents and younger sister. At home, his family continues to speak their first language (not English); Peter, however, has a grade-appropriate knowledge of English and is able to speak the language without trouble. With his family, Peter speaks comfortably and is described as having a great sense of humor. But Peter's parents describe him as a boy who has always been shy and slow to warm up to unfamiliar people or situations. Although he had one special neighborhood friend during his early childhood, Peter has been unsuccessful in developing new friendships since his move to this country. Peter tends to spend most of his free time alone in his bedroom playing computer games. He doesn't participate in any organized extracurricular activities and his family tends to prefer time spent together or with extended family. Peter's father can relate to his son's situation, as he recalls being a painfully shy boy, and he still feels uncomfortable in social situations.

At school, Peter tends to keep to himself and spends most lunch and recess times doing homework. He does not speak to any of the other students at school, although he manages to interact nonverbally with them during group projects or class assignments. Peter excels in all subject areas and is motivated to achieve good grades. In recent years, Peter has started to speak one-on-one to his teachers but only if it is necessary in evaluation situations—for example, to ask about an assignment or to show his reading skills when required. In those rare situations, Peter limits his speaking, uses a quiet voice, and speaks only when away from his peers.

These two examples of children with selective mutism demonstrate how a fear of speaking can affect a child's life in different ways. Although children with selective mutism tend to have some things in common, the unique qualities and experiences of each child can lead to different types of challenges. In the pages that follow, we'll share general information that will allow you to better understand and help your child work through this often misunderstood condition.

1

What Is Selective Mutism?

CHAPTER OBJECTIVES

In this chapter you will learn the following:

★ Some common characteristics of selective mutism

★ When selective mutism starts

★ How common selective mutism is

★ How well children with selective mutism get along with peers

★ How selective mutism affects children's academic development

★ Whether selective mutism impacts children's self-esteem

★ How long selective mutism persists

★ Some difficulties associated with selective mutism

COMMON CHARACTERISTICS OF SELECTIVE MUTISM

Children who have selective mutism do not speak in some situations. While children with selective mutism are typically comfortable speaking at home, they often do not talk freely at school. Most parents describe a child who is "a completely different kid" at home in comparison to the way he acts at school. Perhaps your child is like Sarah, described by her mother as very quiet at school yet a chatterbox at home. Some parents even say that they wish their child spoke a little less at home—something that teachers of children with selective mutism often have trouble imagining.

While children who have selective mutism usually speak comfortably and at a normal volume at home or in other familiar settings, they often do not speak to teachers, other students, principals, or school secretaries. In addition, many children with selective mutism go through a period when they do not speak to anyone at school, typically around the time the condition first appears. When asked to speak, they often look down, blush, and show other signs of anxiety.

Like Sarah and Peter, who were discussed in the introduction, children with selective mutism often interact nonverbally with their classmates. They do so through gesturing, pointing, and nodding, but they draw the line at making any audible sound, such as laughing. Reports from parents and teachers suggest that children with selective mutism become highly skilled at making their wishes and needs known without ever saying a word.

Selective Mutism Is Viewed as a Specific Phobia

Many experts believe that children with selective mutism have a *specific phobia*. A specific phobia is an excessive fear that is limited to the presence or anticipation of a particular situation or thing. In the case of selective mutism, the child has a specific fear of being heard or seen speaking in certain situations. This particular type of phobia, in fact, may have much in common with other specific phobias, such as the fear of heights, water, snakes, spiders, or strangers. Research suggests that we may all be physiologically prepared to acquire fears that hold some protective value (for example, Hofmann, Moscovitch, and Heinrichs 2003). It makes sense to be cautious in frightening situations that are perceived to be potentially threatening or dangerous. For the child with selective mutism, entering an unfamiliar setting like school or day care with unfamiliar people may seem threatening or dangerous. Other research has indicated that, around the same age that selective mutism typically first appears, specific fears or phobias are very common among preschool-aged children (Ollendick, King, and Muris 2002). From this line of thinking, selective mutism can be considered a specific form of phobia that emerges in response to any number of factors, which we will look at more closely in chapter 2.

THE IMPORTANCE OF LOCATION, PEOPLE, AND ACTIVITIES

At this point, you might be wondering why your child is able to speak in some situations and to some people, but not others. The extent to which children with selective mutism speak or even participate nonverbally often varies depending on the circumstances and the child's comfort levels. Some of the factors that seem to make a difference for these children include the specifics of the setting, such as the people involved and the activity taking place. Let's consider some of the more common patterns of speaking shown by children with selective mutism according to three factors: location, people, and activities. As you read this next section, think about how each factor applies to your child.

Location. Research has shown that children who have selective mutism are most likely to speak at home, less likely to speak outside of the home (for example, at the grocery store), and least likely to speak at school (Black and Uhde 1995; Cunningham et al. 2004). For a variety of reasons, the school setting is particularly anxiety-provoking for these children. If we consider that many children have at least some difficulty making the adjustment to starting school, and add to that the fact that they're shy or have trouble speaking, it's not difficult to understand how going to school can be a very stressful experience. In our clinical work, we often hear parents describing times when they had considerable difficulty getting their child to go to school in the morning. Other parents tell us that their child likes going off to school and enjoys the day, despite being silent. How does your child react to the school setting?

Many children who have selective mutism are so sensitive to their surroundings that their speaking varies even within the school setting. Our clinical experience suggests that children with selective mutism are most likely to first speak at school in situations that are more private, are visually different from the classroom setting, and have not been associated with a pressure to speak. For instance, children with selective mutism often feel more comfortable while on the school playground or in the gymnasium (perhaps enough to even say a few words) than they are in the classroom. In the example given in the introduction, Sarah speaks to her classmate only when they are on the school playground and out of the earshot of other children or teachers, but not in the classroom or hallway. Similarly, there are probably locations in the classroom that provoke less anxiety than others. So, as Sarah becomes more comfortable speaking at school, she will likely begin talking to her friend in a quiet corner near the back of the classroom before she would speak to this same friend at the front of the classroom, by the teacher's desk, for example.

People. Typically, children with selective mutism are more likely to speak to other children than to adults. Again, this is illustrated by Sarah's example. In contrast, in a much smaller number of cases, certain children with selective mutism speak to adults first. This is true for Peter, who will speak one-on-one to teachers if doing so will improve his grades. For Peter, in specific situations like teacher evaluations, his motivation to excel academically seems to override his fear of being seen or heard speaking.

Family and friends. Children with selective mutism may have difficulty speaking to neighbors, relatives, or unfamiliar adults. Some children will not say a word to grandparents or other close family members, much to their parents' dismay. It is also not unusual for these children to whisper to their babysitter or simply shut down when the family doctor or dentist tries to engage them in small talk. In contrast, other children with selective mutism have no difficulty speaking with strangers in public. For these children, the fear of being seen or heard speaking is quite specific to school and to situations involving those people who know about their mutism.

Strangers. Within the school setting, strangers are often the first to hear the child speak aloud. We have heard many stories from surprised parents who have discovered that their child spoke for the first time at school—to a new student teacher or parent volunteer. Despite the child's familiarity with the classroom teacher, other school personnel, and classmates, an anxiety-based behavioral pattern has developed between the child with selective mutism and these individuals.

If your child feels anxious about speaking to a particular person, he'll likely be nervous about speaking to that same person in the future. For example, we know of children who have worked through their selective mutism but several years later still felt too anxious to speak to a previous teacher. It is as if the earlier pattern of not speaking, and the experience of anxiety when speaking to the teacher, has remained unchanged. Does your child's comfort level when speaking vary depending on the people involved?

Teachers. In most cases, the teacher is one of the last people to hear the child with selective mutism speak. The child's reaction to the teacher typically has less to do with the teacher's personality or instructional style than with what that person represents: an authority figure whose job is to evaluate the child's performance, most typically through oral expression. As with locations, many children are sensitive to subtle differences in the people involved and their relationship to them. For example, they might first speak to an educational assistant or librarian before they would risk speaking to the regular classroom teacher.

Activities. Although scientists have not yet examined the types of activities children with selective mutism find the least anxiety-provoking, our clinical experience points to some possibilities. First, children with selective mutism seem more likely to speak during activities where they have tended to speak in the past. So, you may want to try to involve your child in these kinds of activities (for example, ask your child to play "Old Maid" or a similar game if he tends to be chatty while playing card games). Also, when considering activities for your child, think about how much speaking the activity requires. If your goal is to promote speaking, playing video games or silent reading might not be good choices, because these activities do not involve much talking.

Another thing to think about when choosing activities for your child is how comfortable and enjoyable the activity is for your child. Playing a favorite board game might be a good choice, or perhaps your child would prefer pretend play with a much-loved toy. Try to think of activities that encourage fun and laughter, because your child is less likely to feel self-conscious about speaking when feeling relaxed and having a great time. Parents of children who enjoy physical, sports-related activities often report that their children are more likely to speak when they are outside running around, instead of sitting still. Activities that are more structured and are similar to class assignments, such as reading or completing written exercises, are usually less likely to promote comfortable speaking in the beginning stages.

More Than a Fear of Speaking

Many children who have selective mutism not only restrict their talking in settings such as school but are inhibited in other ways too. Perhaps your child tends to be hesitant during group activities, team sports, or free play, preferring to watch from the sidelines. Some parents and teachers describe a child who is a keen, interested observer of social interaction, but an unwilling participant. Some children physically shut down or appear frozen in their steps. They may refuse to participate in physical education, even when some of these activities might be favorites at home or with a few close friends in the neighborhood. A smaller number of children are so physically restricted and self-conscious that they will not eat in front of others or will avoid using the bathroom at school. Maybe these descriptions do not fit your child. Perhaps your child instead seems comfortable in school situations as long as speaking is not required. The degree of inhibition can vary greatly not only in situations where speaking is required but in activities that don't require speaking as well.

The Conversational Ladder

Despite differences in speaking patterns between children, for each child with selective mutism there is usually a definite ladder, or hierarchy, of situations in which the child feels progressively more uncomfortable speaking. This hierarchy ranges from those situations in which the child currently speaks comfortably to those in which the child is not yet ready to speak.

Table 1 describes the stages in which speaking tends to emerge for children who have selective mutism. Of course, there are no hard-and-fast rules. No two children are the same, and so no two children with selective mutism can be expected to progress in exactly the same way or at the same pace. Nonetheless, these ten stages outline the way in which many children overcome their difficulty speaking in anxiety-provoking settings.

As you read this section, identify those people with whom your child currently speaks, the locations where he currently speaks, and the activities that most often encourage him to speak. If you put all of this information together, you can develop a "ladder" to roughly sequence the steps in which your own child will work toward more comfortable speaking. You've probably witnessed just how unwilling your child can be when asked to speak beyond his current stage or comfort level. In chapter 7, you'll have the opportunity to identify the steps your child will need to work through to progress toward more comfortable speaking.

Developing comfort with speaking at school		
Stage	Description	Age at which your child reached this stage
1. Complete mutism at school	Child speaks at home but is silent at school. Appears anxious at school and may resist attending school.	
2. Relaxed nonverbal participation	Child speaks at home but not at school. Begins relaxing and participating nonverbally in classroom activities. May begin to talk positively about school.	

3. Speaks to parent at school	Child speaks at school when alone with parent in a place where students and teachers cannot hear or see, often in a whispered voice.	
4. Speaking observed by peers	Child speaks at school, usually to a parent. Peers observe but do not hear the child speaking, since he typically whispers so quietly as to be inaudible to observers.	
5. Speaking overheard by peers	Child speaks audibly at school, usually to a parent. Other children observe and hear the child speaking. Child does not speak directly to other children or teachers.	
6. Speaking through parent to peers	Child speaks to parent, who conveys message to another classmate sitting nearby. The classmate may overhear the child with selective mutism speaking and respond directly.	
7. Speaking to peers	Child speaks at school to one peer, often on the playground. Child does not speak to teachers.	
8. Speaking to several peers	Child speaks to several children at school. Child does not speak to teachers.	
9. Speaking to teacher	Child begins speaking to teacher and speaks to several peers.	
10. Normal speaking	Child speaks to most adults and peers in a normal conversational tone.	

Exercise 1.1 Identifying Your Child's Step on the Ladder

Now, take a moment and think about when your own child reached each stage. How old was he and what grade was he in? What stage would you say your child is at right now? Record your observations in a separate notebook or journal that you'll keep just for the purpose of working through this book.

Remember that children with selective mutism tend to work very gradually through the stages toward speaking comfortably. At this point in the book, most parents are likely to find that their child is at stage one or two. If your child has begun to make some gains in working through his selective mutism, you may find him to be a little further along, perhaps at stage three, four, or even five. It's important to have a sense of where your child currently is on the ladder so that you have an idea of what he needs to work toward next. The many strategies that you'll learn about in chapters 4 through 9 of this book can be of assistance to your child, regardless of his current stage. You might want to mark this page in your notebook so that you can easily refer to it as you work through this book. We encourage you to come back to your stages chart and add your child's newest achievements as he progresses, with your help.

WHEN DOES SELECTIVE MUTISM BEGIN?

When gathering background information about the clients we serve, we routinely ask parents about the age at which their child began to speak selectively. They typically respond by saying that their child has always been this way. Research supports these comments. Selective mutism typically appears when children are two to five years old (Black and Uhde 1995; Cunningham et al. 2004). However, a diagnosis is usually not made or treatment is not sought until children are six to eight years old (for example, Remschmidt et al. 2001). So what accounts for this delay? One reason is that it can be difficult for parents and professionals to distinguish selective mutism from more general shyness. Because of this, many parents and professionals consider children with selective mutism to be just shy and view their reluctance to speak as a phase they will outgrow. Also, many preschoolers with selective mutism are comfortable speaking at home to familiar people. So, their discomfort with speaking in less-familiar settings may not become noticeable until they first enter day care or school.

While many children who are reluctant to speak at school are correctly identified as having selective mutism during kindergarten or first grade, others are not. Starting school is a time of adjustment for many children, who may act shy at times as they warm up to the new school setting. Many parents and professionals expect that the young child will outgrow the mutism. This is not an unreasonable assumption, for many children do in fact begin speaking comfortably after they adjust to school life. Unfortunately, though, some children continue to be mute long after other children in the class have made the adjustment.

HOW COMMON IS SELECTIVE MUTISM?

Before you picked up this book or spoke to a professional, the term *selective mutism* might have been completely new to you. If this is true, you're not alone. Most parents have not heard of this condition, and many wonder if their child is the only one going through this. Rest assured that your child is not the only person facing the fear of being seen or heard speaking. Although selective mutism was originally thought to be very rare, recent research suggests that this condition occurs in up to 2 percent of children in early elementary school (Kumpulainen et al. 1998). While it is certainly not as common as other children's difficulties, like attention-deficit/hyperactivity disorder (ADHD) or certain learning disabilities, the numbers suggest that a significant number of children are affected by selective mutism. This condition seems to occur about one and a half to two times more often in girls than in boys (for example, Steinhausen and Juzi 1996).

HOW DO OTHER CHILDREN REACT TO STUDENTS WITH SELECTIVE MUTISM?

Children with selective mutism usually develop friendships with neighborhood peers and often some classmates. This may surprise you, because we adults may find it hard to imagine how a friendship can be formed with someone who doesn't answer your questions, give you compliments, or laugh out loud at your jokes. Yet young children seem comfortable interacting nonverbally, even with a peer who has never spoken to them. Like Sarah, children who have selective mutism are usually well liked by their peers. The fact that many children with selective mutism form friendships with at least a small group of peers is important, since it shows that certain aspects of their social development appear to be normal, and that peer relationships are just as important for their development as they are for typical children. Other children with selective mutism, like Peter, spend less time with peers and so they have fewer opportunities to practice comfortable speaking and other social skills.

Within the classroom, it's not unusual for classmates to actually speak for the child with selective mutism. Certain peers often nominate themselves to be a spokesperson, speaking on behalf of the child or informing those new to the classroom that the child doesn't talk. Other peers, particularly in the earlier grades, may take on a nurturing, caregiving role with the child who has selective mutism.

Some parents wonder whether their child will be teased or bullied. It's understandable that you might have these concerns, especially because the research shows that shy children are at greater risk for victimization by peers (for example, Boivin, Hymel, and Bukowski 1995). However, the limited research on this topic suggests that children with selective mutism are not more likely to be teased or bullied than their peers (Cunningham et al. 2004). Only about 5 percent of children with selective mutism are estimated to be bullied by peers (Kumpulainen et al. 1998), while up to 19 percent of the general population of American elementary school children are bullied (Pellegrini, Bartini, and Brooks 2001). Although these findings may be surprising to you, remember that by saying nothing your child doesn't risk saying anything offensive to his peers. Also, children who have selective mutism don't display the kind of disruptive behavior often seen in children who are victimized by peers.

This is not to say, however, that children who have selective mutism are competent in all social situations. As a parent of a child who does not speak in some situations, you know firsthand what a struggle it can be for your child to make his needs and wishes known. In one recent study, both parents and teachers reported that children with selective mutism were less assertive than their peers in situations that called for speaking (Cunningham et al. 2004)—naturally, they are less likely to join a group, introduce themselves, start conversations, or invite friends to their house.

Exercise 1.2   How Schoolmates React to Your Child

Take out your notebook or journal. Think about what you've heard from your own child or the school's staff, or maybe what you've seen yourself with regard to how other children get along with your child. Here are some questions to consider:

Does your child have one or two special friends at school?

Is there at least one classmate who is known to look out for your child and take on a caregiving role?

In general, is your child able to join in the play of his peers?

Can he introduce himself, start a conversation, or invite a friend to your home for a playdate?

To date, has your child ever been teased or bullied by his classmates?

Has your child had particular trouble getting along with another child from school?

Do other children help your child in activities that require speaking?

In later chapters, we'll introduce to you specific things you can do to help your child become more comfortable and skilled in social situations that present a challenge to him.

HOW DO CHILDREN WITH SELECTIVE MUTISM DO ACADEMICALLY?

Selective mutism does not necessarily interfere with academic development. In the early grades, children with selective mutism typically acquire reading, math, and written language skills at a rate that would be expected given their intellectual abilities. Despite the worries of parents and school personnel, academic progress doesn't seem to be significantly hampered by a child's discomfort with speaking in certain school situations. Indeed, our own research has shown that, when young children with selective mutism are tested at home, their math and reading abilities do not differ from those of typical children (Cunningham et al. 2004). In fact, we know of one child with selective mutism who even won the reading excellence award for the entire county! However, less is known about the impact of persistent selective mutism on the academic development of older children.

Some parents might wonder how it's possible for young children with selective mutism to excel academically, given the important role that oral communication plays in the classroom. Research suggests that some factors may protect children with selective mutism from academic struggles. For one thing, children who have selective mutism are rated as just as competent as their classmates in various nonverbal behaviors that are essential to academic success, including attending to instructions, following directions, managing transitions between activities, finishing assignments on time, producing correct work, waiting for help, and ignoring peer distractions. Children who have selective mutism also show fewer acting-out behaviors than their classmates, which often contribute to learning difficulties. These factors, among others, may allow children with selective mutism to perform to their capabilities in the classroom, even without speaking (Cunningham et al. 2004).

Despite all this, selective mutism can make it very difficult for educators to assess children's knowledge and learning. Teachers are often unsure how to evaluate the academic skills of these children, particularly in the areas of language and oral reading. Some parents worry that teachers might underestimate the skills of a child who doesn't speak in the classroom. If your child's teachers are having difficulty evaluating his academic skills, see chapter 10 for some creative ways teachers can assess his skills in areas that require oral communication, like reading fluency and oral presentations.

WILL SELECTIVE MUTISM AFFECT YOUR CHILD'S SELF-ESTEEM?

A very common concern among parents, and a completely under-standable one at that, is whether selective mutism will affect their child's self-esteem. Some parents worry that their children will feel poorly about themselves because of selective mutism. Do you feel that your child lacks confidence because of his struggles with mutism?

Rest assured that, to date, no research evidence has suggested that children with selective mutism have lower self-esteem than their peers. However, it's important that you monitor your child's sense of self and offer positive feedback regarding his strengths and special qualities. Given your child's specific difficulties with speaking in certain situations, you'll need to encourage a sense of mastery and competence in other areas. Tips for helping your child feel more confident and skilled will be introduced throughout this book.

HOW LONG DOES SELECTIVE MUTISM LAST?

The course of selective mutism can vary from one child to the next. Some children who are hesitant to speak when they first start school or day care may speak comfortably by the end of that same year without any special supports. Others may continue to experience difficulty beyond the first year. With the introduction of effective strategies like those you'll see in this book, some children can work through selective mutism in one to two years. Persistent selective mutism is less common, but in the absence of effective intervention it can last through primary, middle, and in some cases the high school years. The key seems to be to intervene early; the sooner your child is helped to work through his fear of speaking, the better.

Even though most children with selective mutism learn to cope with their anxiety and begin to speak in more settings, it seems that many continue to feel shy or anxious in social situations. Only a few research studies have followed children with selective mutism into adolescence and adulthood. This research revealed that nearly half of adolescents and adults who had received treatment for selective mutism as a child reported no current difficulties. The other half characterized themselves as less self-confident, less independent, and less mature than others their age who didn't have a history of selective mutism (Remschmidt et al. 2001).

WHAT OTHER DIFFICULTIES ARE ASSOCIATED WITH SELECTIVE MUTISM?

If you've read some of the literature on selective mutism, you've probably noticed that many emotional and behavioral problems are described as sometimes occurring alongside this condition. Below, we'll briefly consider the scientific evidence for the most commonly cited problems, including other anxiety-related issues, hesitancy to use school bathrooms, and oppositional behavior. As you read through this section, think about whether your child experiences any or all of these problems.

Other Anxiety-Related Issues

Many children with selective mutism become fearful or anxious not only in situations where speaking is involved but in other circumstances as well. Numerous researchers have found children with selective mutism to be generally more anxious than other children their age (for example, Dummit et al. 1997), and there seems to be a higher rate of anxiety disorders among children who have selective mutism. In fact, research has shown that most children with selective mutism could also be diagnosed with at least one other anxiety-related problem (Bergman, Piacentini, and McCracken 2002). The most common anxiety problems include social phobia, separation anxiety, and perfectionistic or obsessive tendencies.

SOCIAL PHOBIA

Of all the psychological problems identified as often occurring with selective mutism, social phobia appears to be the most common among these children. Children who show symptoms of social phobia have an intense fear of negative evaluation by others and are overly concerned that they might say or do something to embarrass themselves. A significant number of the children with selective mutism we see in our clinical work not only restrict their use of speech but are socially inhibited in other ways as well. As we mentioned earlier, some children avoid playing with peers, refuse to eat in front of others, or even avoid using public bathrooms. The fear of embarrassing themselves prevents these children from socially engaging with the world beyond a small number of highly familiar, and thus safe, individuals.

Some research suggests that a large proportion of children with selective mutism also have social phobia (Black and Uhde 1995; Dummit et al. 1997). However, other research suggests that very few children with social phobia also have characteristics of selective mutism (Beidel, Turner, and Morris 1999). The way these two conditions are related has yet to be clearly sorted out. Although there may indeed be some overlap between them, there are also important differences. For example, as we mentioned earlier, selective mutism tends to first appear between the ages of two and four. Social phobia doesn't usually first appear until a child is older, around ten or eleven years of age. Similarly, whereas a child with selective mutism may interact comfortably with others through nonverbal means, this isn't typical of a child with social phobia, who will tend to be anxious about all aspects of social interaction.

Remember this: Your child's anxious tendencies may be limited to a fear of speaking and he may be quite comfortable spending time with others as long as he doesn't have to speak. But it is also possible that your child is anxious in social situations with others even when no talking is required. For this reason, it's important for you to monitor your child's level of comfort while interacting with peers so you can determine whether he is also experiencing anxiety in social situations in general.

SEPARATION ANXIETY

Some parents of children with selective mutism characterize their child as becoming anxious at the thought of separating from them, even for a brief period of time. This description is supported by evidence: Some researchers have found that a number of children with selective mutism also have separation anxiety issues. While some children with selective mutism have difficulties separating from their parent(s) to attend school, others have additional problems with separation, such as reluctance to sleep in a different room from parent(s), and worry that something bad will happen to them or to a loved one. Separation issues that are significant enough to warrant a diagnosis of separation anxiety disorder have been reported in approximately 20 to 30 percent of children who have selective mutism (Kristensen 2000; Steinhausen and Juzi 1996).

PERFECTIONISTIC OR OBSESSIVE TENDENCIES

Some parents of children with selective mutism also report more perfectionistic or obsessive symptoms in their children than parents of children without selective mutism do. Obsessions are persistent thoughts or ideas that can be associated with anxiety or distress, leading a person to believe their surroundings need to be a certain way (for example, they are particular about having everything in place), or causing them to be overly concerned with making mistakes (for example, they are meticulous when completing schoolwork).

FEAR OF USING SCHOOL BATHROOMS

In our work with children who have selective mutism, parents sometimes tell us that their child is hesitant to use the bathroom at school. Of course, this might be related to a fear of asking the teacher, since gaining permission to use the bathroom often involves raising your hand, making the request, and drawing attention to yourself in the process. Each of these steps can be very anxiety-provoking for a child with selective mutism. We sometimes hear from parents and teachers that children with selective mutism don't use the bathroom all day while at school and then are desperate to use the bathroom as soon as they get home. It's easy to see how wetting accidents might occur given these circumstances. It's unclear at this point why some children with selective mutism are also afraid to use public bathrooms in the community. These children may be experiencing a more general social phobia. As noted above, many children who have social phobia are reluctant to use public bathrooms anywhere.

Oppositional Behavior

Certain research studies report that oppositional behavior is fairly common among children with selective mutism (Kristensen 2001; Kumpulainen et al. 1998). The children studied were described by their parents as more stubborn, defiant, manipulative, and demanding than other children. In contrast, other research studies have found no behavior differences between children with and without selective mutism based on parent reports (for example,

Dummit et al. 1997). It's of interest to note that teachers report fewer disruptive behaviors (such as oppositional tendencies) at school than parents do at home (Cunningham et al. 2004). Of course, this makes sense, since teachers would naturally observe fewer disruptive verbal behaviors in these children than their parents do, given that most children who have selective mutism don't speak freely at school.

When faced with silent demonstrations of defiance, teachers may describe these children as strong-willed, digging in their heels and refusing to comply with classroom instructions, especially if these instructions require the child to take risks, speech related or otherwise. However, many professionals in this area contend that a failure to follow instructions or noncompliance serves the purpose of helping the child with selective mutism avoid feared situations. Research may support this notion: Although a minority of children with selective mutism display defiance, these children don't typically act this way in the absence of anxiety (Dummit et al. 1997). Their behavior might appear defiant, controlling, or manipulative, but the evidence suggests it's most likely anxiety based rather than willful noncompliance.

Exercise 1.3   What Characteristics of Selective Mutism Apply to Your Child?

Take a moment to review the common characteristics of selective mutism, and the difficulties often associated with it, presented in this chapter. Which one(s) do you think apply to your child's situation? Write your thoughts in your notebook or journal.

- Speaks in some settings/situations but not others
- Relies on nonverbal communication (for example, gestures like pointing) in some situations
- Can become physically frozen at times
- Shows signs of other anxiety-related issues, like social phobia, separation anxiety, and/or perfectionistic or obsessive tendencies
- Shows a hesitancy to use school bathrooms
- Displays defiant or stubborn behavior

2

Why Does Selective Mutism Happen?

CHAPTER OBJECTIVES

In this chapter you will learn the following:

★ Possible factors contributing to the emergence of selective mutism

★ How to critically examine common misconceptions about selective mutism

FIVE FACTORS THAT MAY CONTRIBUTE TO SELECTIVE MUTISM

Scientists do not yet know what causes selective mutism. However, some factors seem to contribute to, or at least occur along with, selective mutism, including those listed below:

■ A shy or anxious temperament

■ A family history of shyness or anxiety

■ Speech or language difficulties

■ Adjustment to a new culture

■ Limited socializing with school peers away from school

As you read through the descriptions of these factors, think about which, if any, relate to your child's circumstances. At the end of the chapter, you'll be asked to take out your notebook or journal to record the factors that are relevant to your own child.

A Shy or Anxious Temperament

Like Peter, whom we described in the introduction, many children with selective mutism are shy and "slow to warm up" in unfamiliar circumstances. As discussed in chapter 1, parents often say their child has always been shy. The following are some other common descriptors used in connection with these children: sensitive, hesitant, timid, and frightened (the last especially when faced with new situations or new people).

Shyness and social phobia (as described in greater detail in chapter 1) are so often seen in children who have selective mutism that over the last fifteen years some scientists have begun to question whether selective mutism should even be thought of as a condition separate from social anxiety. These scientists believe that selective mutism might simply be a symptom or form of a social phobia, contending that children's social anxiety falls along a continuum, with selective mutism reflecting the most extreme form (Dummit et al. 1997). They believe it's merely an issue of severity: children with selective mutism are simply more anxious about speaking in feared situations than other children, who may become nervous when expected to speak in social situations but still say at least a few words. This debate will likely continue for some time, and certainly more research is needed to determine if scientists should continue to think of selective mutism as separate from, albeit highly related to, social phobia.

The very shy, slow-to-warm-up child may panic when asked to talk at school. This anxiety then becomes associated with the classroom, teacher, students, and school in general. In an attempt to manage this anxiety and gain some control over the situation, the child remains silent. You may have come across the term *behavioral inhibition* in your reading about selective mutism. Behaviorally inhibited children are said to display behavioral inhibition when they show limited behavioral and verbal activity. For example, six-year-old Danny freezes in his steps and doesn't move or say a word when he becomes overwhelmed by anxiety. This freeze response is a basic human reaction in the face of real, or even perceived, danger. Behavioral inhibition helps to reduce the fear somewhat, and so children use this in an attempt to manage their response in anxiety-provoking situations. Over time, given the fact that anxiety reduction can be reinforcing, the child with selective mutism develops a habit of not speaking, and she begins to use it as a coping strategy. It's this habit that you'll work to gradually change, using the steps outlined in later chapters.

One common way that people in general cope with overwhelming anxiety is to avoid the feared situation. Lisa, an eight-year-old child with selective mutism, uses avoidance behavior every time she stands against the school building during recess in order to avoid socializing with other children. Your own child might cope with fearful situations by not attending a classmate's birthday party or by asking to stay home from school. (Clearly, attending school is necessary, and children experiencing anxiety can be difficult to persuade; if your child is refusing to go to school, see chapter 12 for some parenting tips on dealing with an anxious child.)

A Family History of Shyness or Anxiety

Often, one or both parents report a family history of temperament or personality characteristics similar to those shown by their child, including shyness, anxiety, social phobia, and selective mutism. Perhaps a cousin or uncle had a similar early history or is still viewed as very quiet at family functions. Many parents tell us that they too can identify with their child's experience, having been shy themselves as children. We see this in the case of Peter, whose father remembers being very shy as a boy. Perhaps you were shy and reluctant to talk in new situations or to unfamiliar adults when you were young. Maybe, like Peter's father, you still find it difficult to "be yourself" in some social situations. Maybe you sometimes worry that your words might not come out right or that others will get a negative impression of you. Of course, if you did have these worries, you wouldn't be alone. Many adults experience shyness in social situations, and a great many also feel uncomfortable speaking in public.

Although research suggests that anxiety disorders tend to run in families of children with selective mutism (for example, Kristensen and Torgensen 2001), it's not known whether children take on their parents' anxious tendencies by way of genetic or situational factors or, more likely, some combination of the two. It's by no means a clear-cut issue, for some children who have selective mutism come from sociable, easygoing families. But even if you're convinced that your child takes after you or her other parent, is that a reason to blame yourself? Certainly not. First of all, at the present time, we have no way of knowing for sure that your child inherited shyness or anxiety from you. Second, current knowledge suggests that selective mutism doesn't have any single cause; it's more complicated than that. Third, at this point, no research evidence suggests that any particular type of parenting contributes to the emergence of selective mutism. In fact, in our own research, we've looked at parenting styles (for example, methods of discipline) and other family characteristics, such as relationship and communication styles. We found no difference when we compared parents of children with selective mutism to parents of children without selective mutism (Cunningham et al. 2004).

What we do know from working with many parents is that you can use your parenting skills to help your child overcome selective mutism. As a parent, you play a very important role in helping your child become more comfortable speaking in a range of situations and to various people. In later chapters we suggest some actions that you can take to help your child become more confident when speaking.

Speech or Language Difficulties

It's not hard to imagine why children who have speech or language difficulties would be hesitant to talk. In their minds, not saying anything at all prevents others from hearing their less-than-perfect speech and hence eliminates any chance that they might be ridiculed for the way they talk. Indeed, some research shows that children who have selective mutism may also have speech and language difficulties or a history of delayed language development (Kristensen 2000; Steinhausen and Juzi 1996). Some of the difficulties described by researchers in the field include delayed onset of speech, stuttering, and articulation problems. An early history of speech or language problems does not necessarily mean a child will always have these difficulties. For some children, speech and language therapy may be helpful. For others, early problems simply lessen as they grow older.

What remains unclear is whether in fact children with selective mutism are more likely to have speech and language difficulties than other children. This is an important research question that needs to be addressed more carefully. As you might imagine, it's a challenge to assess the speech and language skills of a child who may feel anxious, inhibited, and uncomfortable talking outside of the home. Conventional assessment approaches, such as examining a sample of the child's oral language or asking the child to orally answer questions, need to be modified in specialized ways for the child with selective mutism. Your child may be experiencing speech or language difficulties that you'll want to have assessed. We will talk further about this in chapter 3 when we look at the potential role of a speech and language assessment in helping your child.

Adjustment to a New Culture

For some children, adjusting to a new culture seems to contribute to the emergence of selective mutism. Research shows a higher prevalence of the condition among immigrant children (for example, Elizur and Perednik 2003). As you might imagine, school can be a highly stressful experience for recently immigrated children, particularly for children from families who speak a language different from the one spoken at school, and for those who practice different customs from those at school. For these children, adjusting to school means not only meeting new children and teachers but also adjusting to a new language, culture, and so forth. This is the case for Peter, discussed in the introduction, whose parents speak their first language at home. This adjustment isn't limited to children whose families have recently immigrated, however. Children who attend language-immersion schools would also fit into this group.

Limited Socializing with School Peers Away from School

Families who are socially or geographically isolated may be more at risk of having a child with selective mutism. In our clinical work with these children, we often hear from parents that their child's friends do not attend the same class or even the same school. Frequently, the child with selective mutism has neighborhood friends and maybe some school friends, but they rarely overlap. For instance, Lisa takes the bus to school and lives in a different area than her classmates, so geographical distance plays a role in her social isolation. Danny lives in the same neighborhood as his classmates, but he doesn't get together to play with these kids, since his parents don't know the neighborhood families and can't contact them to arrange playdates. Some children with selective mutism, like Peter, tend to play only with children who are in their family, such as siblings or cousins, or who share their language and customs. Some families are simply not very socially or community oriented, preferring to spend their time engaged in more solitary or family-based activities.

Do any of these descriptions fit your family circumstances? If so, you may want to provide opportunities for your child to play—at your home—with classmates from the school. In chapter 9, we offer some suggestions for doing just that.

HOW THESE FACTORS CAN COMBINE IN VARIOUS WAYS

Most children with selective mutism have been influenced by more than one of the above-mentioned factors. Like many other childhood psychological conditions, selective mutism appears to be caused by the combined effects of the child's temperament and circumstances in her environment. Indeed, it's our clinical experience that parents of children with selective mutism typically acknowledge that several of these contributing factors may be at play in their child's case.

If a family history of shyness and anxiety is present in addition to the child's natural tendency toward shyness, there are likely fewer individuals in the child's life to serve as models of assertive or sociable behavior. A child with this combination of factors might instead learn to imitate shy, anxious behavior, and as a result the shy tendencies could become more deeply ingrained personality traits.

A child who is predisposed to be shy would likely become even more anxious when faced with socializing in a different language or culture. Children who are shy by nature and do not have strong peer connections between home and school may also be less willing to speak to classmates—children whom they associate only within the anxiety-provoking school setting.

DO TRAUMATIC EVENTS OR FAMILY PROBLEMS CAUSE SELECTIVE MUTISM?

While early trauma and family problems have been suggested as possible contributing factors by some mental health professionals, they've been largely dismissed as primary causes in the development of selective mutism. Let's look at the evidence related to these two factors. Again, as you read, think about whether these issues may play a role in your own child's selective mutism.

Early Trauma

Some professionals in the field contend that highly stressful or traumatic events, such as early hospitalization, the death of a loved one, divorce, and frequent family moves, can lead to the emergence of selective mutism. Several scientists, however, have noted serious flaws in the design of the studies that reported a link between early trauma and selective mutism, and they have set out to test the relationship under more controlled conditions. According to more systematic studies, children who have selective mutism are not more likely than other children to have a history of early trauma or stressful life events (for example, Steinhausen and Juzi 1996). In fact, in one study the researchers didn't find any evidence of trauma among their sample of children with selective mutism (Dummit et al. 1997). As a result of this more recent information, most experts in the field now discount early trauma as a primary contributing factor in the emergence of selective mutism.

This is not to say, of course, that a traumatic event couldn't trigger selective mutism in some children. Certainly, there have been individual cases where children stopped talking shortly after a traumatic event. We don't deny that traumatic experiences might help explain selective mutism in a small percentage of cases. However, the evidence to date shows that trauma doesn't explain why most children with selective mutism develop the condition.

Family Problems

You may also have read that family dysfunction can be a primary cause of selective mutism. According to an early theory, children who have selective mutism are expressing symptoms of dysfunctional family relations. This literature describes the mothers as controlling and overprotective and fathers as inflexible and distant (Hayden 1980). The mother-child relationship is characterized as unhealthy, entangled, and interdependent. The child, it's suggested, learns that the environment and individuals outside the immediate family are not to be trusted, and her silence is explained as an effort to protect family secrets.

However, many of the authors who point to family pathology as a causal factor are simply theorizing and don't have research evidence to support their beliefs. Although there have been some case reports suggesting a link between family dysfunction and selective mutism, evidence from well-designed research studies does not support this relationship (Kristensen 2000). In a recent study we conducted, no differences in the level of family dysfunction were found. We also found no differences in other family characteristics, including marital status, economic resources, or support networks (Cunningham et al. 2004). Other recent research has similarly found no differences on measures of family conflict, expressiveness, and cohesion (Vecchio and Kearney 2005).

It may be the case that some children develop selective mutism partly in response to dysfunction within their family. However, given the lack of meaningful or consistent differences in family functioning in high-quality research studies, we do not believe that this factor applies to most families of children with selective mutism.

IS SELECTIVE MUTISM A CHOICE?

It's certainly understandable that some people in your life might believe your child's selective mutism is due to choices she makes about talking. It can be very challenging to interact with a child who doesn't talk, and the disheartening and frustrating experience of trying to communicate with the child might lead parents, teachers, or other adults to conclude that the silence is a form of manipulation or out-right defiance. After all, your child does talk with relative ease in some situations, so her silence in other situations must be a choice, right? At this point in the book, you likely can anticipate our response to this question. It's our stance, as well as the stance of many other professionals, that a child's mutism is rather a desperate attempt to manage her fear of speaking. As we mentioned earlier in this chapter in our discussion of behavioral inhibition, the withholding of speech is best viewed as a freeze defense, a common reaction to fear. Children who have selective mutism may want to speak, but their fear response prevents them from doing so. We believe it's unfair to say that children with selective mutism choose not to speak—rather, they can't speak because of anxiety.

Exercise 2.1   What Factors Contribute to Your Child's Mutism?

Take a moment to review the contributing factors presented in this chapter. Which one(s) do you think apply to your child's situation? Write your thoughts in a separate notebook or journal.

- A shy or anxious temperament

- A family history of shyness or anxiety

- Speech or language difficulties

- Adjustment to a new culture

- Few friends in the neighborhood or community who are also in my child's class at school

- Early life stressors

- Family stress

3

How Professionals Can Help Your Child

CHAPTER OBJECTIVES

In this chapter you will learn the following:

★ The formal diagnosis of selective mutism

★ Other conditions or issues that may contribute to your child's silence in certain situations

★ Information you can gather in order to assist with assessment and intervention planning

★ Professional approaches to helping children with selective mutism

★ What approach is likely to be most helpful to your child

DOES YOUR CHILD HAVE SELECTIVE MUTISM?

When a child is observed consistently not speaking in specific settings, the most urgent and perplexing question parents often raise is one of identification: "Is this shyness, a phase that my child will outgrow, or something more?" Although the answer to that question is usually straightforward, the process of finding an answer can be frustrating to some parents. Many children's mental health professionals, physicians, and educators have limited experience with this condition. Experienced teachers, for example, tell us that they have never worked with a child with selective mutism. In general, it would seem that relatively few professionals have much experience with this population, and those who have may not be accessible to all families. That being said, there are many able professionals who can help you understand why your child doesn't talk in certain situations.

The primary criterion for a formal diagnosis of selective mutism is a consistent failure to speak in specific social situations where there is an expectation to speak, such as at school. Most children with selective mutism, in contrast, talk comfortably at home to their family members. In order to receive a diagnosis, in accordance with the *Diagnostic and Statistical Manual of Mental Disorders*, fourth edition (American Psychiatric Association 1994), this type of discrepancy in the child's speaking patterns must have persisted for at least one month and must not be limited to the first month of school or day care. Whereas the primary feature of selective mutism is self-evident, the underlying reasons may not be. As information is gathered about your child's reluctance to speak, it's also important to consider possible explanations, contributing factors, and other conditions that may coexist.

WHAT OTHER CONDITIONS SHOULD BE CONSIDERED, AND WHO CAN HELP?

Although there isn't much scientific research available on the subject, we've observed that certain conditions may be likely to co-occur or contribute to your child's mutism. In cooperation with skilled professionals, each of the factors below should be considered.

Speech or Language Difficulties

As we described in chapter 2, researchers suggest that some children with selective mutism may also struggle with speech and language difficulties. As a parent, have you noticed that your child has trouble expressing ideas, even when in a familiar setting such as home? Think about your child's speech and language, both past and present. How old was your child when he first used words, phrases, and sentences to communicate? Did he learn to talk at the same rate as other same-aged children? At present, is your child able to communicate well using words?

If he has speech- or language-related problems such as a speech delay or articulation troubles, a speech-language pathologist may be able to help you, and other professionals involved, understand your child's articulation skills, ability to communicate with words, and ability to make sense of what he hears. A speech-language assessment may also be able to identify ways in which speech or language problems contribute to, or affect, your child's fear of talking in certain settings. In the case of Sarah, her articulation difficulties were identified at preschool age and she benefited from short-term speech therapy.

Hearing Impairment

A small number of children with atypical speech patterns such as mutism may have some sort of hearing impairment. Does your child have difficulty hearing conversations in open spaces or in large groups, such as on the playground or soccer field? If he seems to hear either poorly or inconsistently, then we suggest that you begin by talking to your family physician or pediatrician about your concerns. In general, we recommend that all children with selective mutism be screened for hearing impairment by an audiologist or other qualified professional.

Mental Abilities and Learning Difficulties

Selective mutism has been reported among children with a wide range of mental abilities. In some instances, however, learning difficulties may also exist. If your child doesn't speak freely at school, it will be difficult for teachers to evaluate his academic progress. Do you notice that your child needs extra time to learn new skills or seems to forget things previously learned? It will be important for the professional(s) working with you to consider whether psychological testing is needed, to identify any learning difficulties. An assessment of this kind can help you to better understand the nature of your child's learning troubles and identify strategies to assist him. It may also point to ways in which the learning difficulties contribute to, or affect, your child's fear of speaking in certain settings.

Exercise 3.1   Recording Your Child's Early Developmental History

Use your notebook or journal to record important information about both your child's early speech and language development, and his hearing, learning, and social development. Consider keeping audio or video footage or drawings your child has made at different developmental stages as he grows. Any professionals you work with will be able to make a more accurate assessment if they have access to a detailed record of your child's developmental history.

SPEECH AND LANGUAGE DEVELOPMENT

How old was your child when he first used words, phrases, and sentences?

In comparison to other children of the same age, how well does your child talk or communicate?

In comparison to other children of the same age, how well does your child understand what others are trying to say to him?

In comparison to other children of the same age, how well do others understand what your child is saying?

HEARING

In comparison to other children of the same age, how well does your child hear?

Has your child's hearing been tested? If so, how recently?

Has your child had ear infections? If so, how many?

LEARNING AND MENTAL ABILITIES

In comparison to other children of the same age, how well does your child learn new things?

Does your child need extra practice to learn new things? Does he remember what he has learned over time?

ADAPTIVE SKILLS

In comparison to other children of the same age, how well does your child do everyday self-care tasks, such as eating, dressing, and so on?

SOCIAL DEVELOPMENT

In comparison to other children of the same age, how well does your child get along with other children or adults?

In comparison to other children of the same age, how much does your child show interest in others?

In comparison to other children of the same age, how does your child handle separation from close family members during everyday activities?

Mental Health Conditions

Finally, it's important for the professional(s) you work with to consider your child's general mental well-being, since certain mental health conditions can co-occur with selective mutism. As we described in chapter 1, some children with selective mutism also show signs of social or separation anxiety, for example. In rare instances, mutism can actually be the result of another mental health condition. Serious thought disorders like schizophrenia and pervasive developmental disorder (PDD), and significant delays in a child's general development such as mental retardation can sometimes better account for a child's tendency not to talk in certain situations. In our experience, this doesn't happen often, but it's important to make sure that you identify all issues affecting your child. In most parts of North America, a regulated health professional such as a psychologist, psychiatrist, or physician with training in children's development or mental health would be able to help rule out or identify co-occurring mental health conditions.

Exercise 3.2   Recording Professional Contacts

As a parent, you'll need to keep track of any contacts you have with professionals on your child's behalf. We encourage you to use your notebook or journal to record information about any professionals with whom you or your child have met in connection with the selective mutism. You might write down the full name and title of each professional involved, that person's contact information, and the purpose and date of each appointment. You should also keep any professional reports or documentation in a safe location—you might be asked to share your records with other professionals who work with you and your child.

WHAT INFORMATION SHOULD YOU GATHER ABOUT YOUR CHILD'S MUTISM?

Once the above explanations for the mutism have been considered, ruled out, or professionally evaluated where necessary, related issues tend to become clearer and easier to identify. As is the case with many childhood issues, selective mutism can fall anywhere along a continuum, from mild to severe. Like Peter, some children with selective mutism may remain silent in many different settings, such as at school, in the community, or even when a grandparent visits the home. Other children, like Sarah, may talk in all but a select few situations, such as when she is required to ask the teacher a question or talk in front of the class.

Parents play an important role in the closer examination of a child's tendency to not speak in certain situations. As described previously, you are a historian and primary observer of your child's speech and language development; hearing, learning, and mental abilities; and general mental health. You also have an important role in recording information about the people with whom your child speaks, where your child speaks, and what activities seem to make your child feel more comfortable while speaking. Any observations you can make about where your child does and doesn't speak can be very helpful in the assessment of the condition and the planning of an appropriate intervention.

Exercise 3.3   Recording the History of Your Child's Mutism

Use your notebook or journal to write down when you first noticed your child didn't talk in some situations. When thinking of the history of your child's hesitancy to speak in some situations, you should also consider and write down the following:

1. **Details regarding the age of your child when the mutism first appeared and how it has changed over time.** For example, over time, some children gradually increase the number of people with whom they speak and the places in which they will do so. Other children seem to maintain the same speaking patterns, talking in certain settings but not in others. And a very small number of children actually speak to fewer people over time.

2. **Situational factors associated with changes in your child's speaking patterns.** Can you identify events that took place just before your child first failed to talk—for example, he visited an unfamiliar relative, started day care, or began attending school?

3. **The situations in which your child does or doesn't speak at present.** It's helpful to systematically outline your child's speaking patterns by making a list of (1) the people with whom he speaks, (2) locations where he speaks, and (3) activities that make him more comfortable speaking. In chapter 1, we described how the ability to speak with confidence varies for children with selective mutism in relation to the people, locations, and activities involved in the speaking situation. We also described how children with selective mutism tend to become more comfortable speaking by working up steps on a sort of a   ladder, going from

less-anxiety-provoking to more-anxiety-provoking speaking situations involving the three factors above.

4. **Once you've written down your three lists** (people, locations, and activities) from step 3, you can then combine this information to identify specific situations in which your child does or doesn't speak. To help you to do this, you can use the speaking situations assessment log that follows in Exercise 3.4. You'll notice that you will be recording information about the people, places, and activities where your child does and does not speak, as well as the quality of speech he uses in a variety of situations. When your child speaks, does he always do so at a normal volume, or do you notice that he sometimes whispers? Alternatively, do you ever notice that your child prefers to use nonverbal gestures, such as nodding or pointing? Is your child sensitive to whether or not someone might hear or see him speaking?

As a parent, you know how your child acts in the situations you're often in together, such as at home or at extracurricular activities in the community. In comparison, you may discover that you are unsure whether your child speaks to other people in situations that you don't observe, such as when the parent of a friend says hello in the school hallway, or during a game on the school playground. Because a child with selective mutism can show very different speaking patterns at school, it will be helpful to ask for the observations of the classroom teacher or other adults who are with your child during the day, such as a playground monitor or gym teacher.

Exercise 3.4   Recording Your Child's Speaking Across Situations

Take some time now and fill out the speaking situations assessment log that follows as completely as possible. You'll notice that you are asked to record your child's speaking patterns with parents, siblings, friends, and teachers. You'll probably find that your child responds differently depending on the person involved. Use your notebook or journal to record how your child's speaking varies depending on the person involved.

Speaking situations assessment log

Child's name:

Rater (circle one): Mother Father Teacher Other

Date:

Instructions: Please record how your child speaks in each of the situations listed below by checking the appropriate column.

Situation	Never talks	Whispers privately (others cannot hear)	Whispers privately (others can hear)	Talks normal volume (others cannot hear)	Talks normal volume (others can hear)
At home or in the community:					
To mother alone at home					
To father alone at home					
To brothers or sisters at home					
To his or her parent with a friend present at home					
To friend(s) at home					
Alone to a friend at a friend's house					
To friend's parent at friend's house					
To parent at grocery store					
To clerk at grocery store					

To others during extracurricular activities							
At school:							
To his or her parent on playground							
To his or her parent in hallway or other nonclassroom setting							
To his or her parent alone in class							
To his or her parent with other students in class							
To friend on playground							
To friend in hallway or other nonclassroom setting							
To friend in class							
To teacher on playground							
To teacher in hallway or other nonclassroom setting							
To teacher in class							
In front of class							

Knowing when, where, and with whom your child feels comfortable talking will help you set goals. Recording this information at different times will help you monitor your child's progress—a topic we will discuss further in chapters 6 and 10.

WHAT TREATMENTS ARE USED FOR SELECTIVE MUTISM?

In the past, treatment for selective mutism was considered to be extremely challenging. Some professionals in the field, in fact, viewed the condition as impossible to treat. The primary goal of most treatment approaches is to help children with selective mutism speak to people with whom they didn't previously speak and to speak in situations in which they didn't previously speak. Many different approaches have been developed, including behavioral strategies, individual therapy in various forms, family therapy, and medication. Treatment programs differ, in part due to different beliefs about the underlying cause of mutism.

The effectiveness of most approaches is not known as they have not yet been assessed through high-quality research. Most published studies describe individual examples of treatment of children with selective mutism. In many of these case studies, therapists used a number of different treatment strategies. As a result, it isn't possible to determine why the child's mutism improved. Did the therapist do or say something helpful while meeting with the child? Did parents or teachers change the way they interacted with the child during the course of treatment? Did the child, on his own, gradually get comfortable with talking to a new friend or to children in a new class? The drawback of these studies is that the results were reported without comparing these children to a similar group of children with selective mutism who did not receive the same help. Unfortunately, that makes it difficult to determine whether other children with selective mutism would benefit in the same way. It also makes it hard to know whether other factors (apart from the treatment), such as the severity of the child's condition, might have affected the outcome.

Of the treatment approaches available, behavioral strategies have been most carefully studied and appear to be most promising (Pionek Stone et al. 2002). Medication and cognitive behavioral approaches have also been viewed as helpful in some cases, although we still don't have enough research to confirm their effectiveness. Given that some professionals may suggest medication or cognitive behavioral therapy (CBT) to you, we'd like to give a brief overview of what is known about each of these treatment approaches first. We will then introduce you to behavioral strategies that have been proven effective and that form the basis of our own intervention program, described to you in chapters 4 through 9.

Medication

Some physicians have suggested to parents that medication may be an effective way to treat selective mutism. Although interest in this treatment approach has increased in the past decade, reliable research proving its effectiveness remains unavailable. A particular class of drugs called serotonin reuptake inhibitors (SRIs), used in the treatment of social phobia and other anxiety conditions, has been suggested to be helpful in the treatment of selective mutism (for example, Dummit et al. 1996). However, be advised that the risks and benefits to your child are not yet fully understood.

Cognitive Behavioral Approaches to Treatment

With the link between anxiety and selective mutism becoming more widely recognized, parents may find that professionals recommend treatments found to be effective for other forms of childhood anxiety. As an offshoot of behavioral approaches (see the next section), CBT has gained recognition as being effective in the treatment of anxiety in adults and, more recently, in children (Kendall et al. 2000). In general, this approach integrates behavioral strategies with an added emphasis on the anxious individual's thoughts. A variety of strategies have been developed as a means to help reduce anxiety by changing thinking patterns. Techniques can include, but are not limited to, training an individual to challenge unrealistic thinking, use problem solving, or employ self-talk.

High-quality research on the effectiveness of CBT for children with selective mutism is not yet available. It's important also to realize that characteristics typical of the child with selective mutism can present particular obstacles to this form of treatment. For example, CBT in its conventional form requires the child to talk to a therapist to share thoughts and feelings. If your child is not comfortable talking in certain situations, then it may be difficult for him to talk to a therapist. Also, given that selective mutism tends to appear when the child is quite young, development itself can serve as an obstacle to the effectiveness of CBT. A child's level of cognitive development dictates in part how well he can think in abstract ways, problem solve, use insight, and think flexibly. Most forms of cognitive behavioral therapy require the individual to be able to evaluate and change their own thought processes; essentially, the individual must be capable of advanced cognitive abilities. Do you think your child is capable of this type of thinking? Although levels of cognitive development can vary from one child to another, in our own experience the age at which selective mutism is best treated is earlier than the age at which CBT strategies have been shown to be helpful.

Behavioral Approaches to Treatment

As we've previously noted, to date behavioral approaches have been most carefully researched and have been proven effective in the treatment of selective mutism (Cunningham et al. 1983; Pionek Stone et al. 2002). In general, behavioral approaches place an emphasis on observable behavior and aspects of the environment that may contribute to, or maintain, certain behavior patterns. Behavior is thought to be, in large part, learned in response to one's environment.

Among behavioral strategies that have been developed, exposure and transfer are considered by most experts to be essential components of effective treatment for anxiety-based conditions in children and adults alike. In order to reduce fear and avoidance of fearful situations, an individual must be exposed to the feared situation in order to learn that he can tolerate that situation and manage any anxiety that emerges. Exposure provides opportunities for the individual to practice different ways of coping with the fear, apart from avoidance.

Exposure opportunities are best introduced in gradual steps on a ladder of least- to most-feared situations. In order to ensure a successful climb up the ladder, the professional designing the program makes sure that each of the identified steps is small and begins with circumstances in which fearful behavior does not occur. By starting with situations in which the person is currently successful, he can gradually transfer that mastery behavior to slightly modified situations. Over time and with repeated exposure, an individual can face increasingly anxiety-producing situations with success.

In general, children learn ways to cope with situations that frighten them. As described in chapter 1, in our view most children with selective mutism are responding to a fear of being heard (or seen) speaking in specific situations. As a result, children with selective mutism may learn to avoid situations where they expect to be pressured to speak. For example, they may avoid eye contact with adults who might ask them questions, prefer to play with children who are comfortable interacting nonverbally, or remain quiet and still so they are not noticed by their teachers. Does your child avoid speaking situations by using any of these behaviors? Avoidance behaviors serve to reduce the immediate anxiety tied to speaking situations, and this relief from anxiety increases the likelihood that the avoidance will happen again in the future.

Through the use of proven behavioral strategies, you can help your child work through his fear of speaking by learning, one step at a time, to feel comfortable talking in a broad range of situations. In chapter 4, you'll read about how behavioral principles guide the intervention program we recommend and many of the strategies we'll suggest to you.

4

What Are the Basic Principles of the Program?

CHAPTER OBJECTIVES

In this chapter you will learn the following:

★ The five basic principles underlying our approach to intervention

In chapters 4 through 9 of this book, we'll take you through each step of our systematic intervention program to help children overcome the fear of speaking. Before describing specific intervention strategies, we'd first like to introduce you to the five principles that guide our approach to intervention. That way, when you encounter strategies in subsequent chapters, you'll understand the rationale for the suggestions that accompany them.

PRINCIPLE ONE: BEHAVIOR IS LEARNED THROUGH EXPERIENCE

As we discussed in chapter 2, your child's fear of speaking in certain situations is likely due to some combination of temperament and environmental factors. Although your child's inherited temperament or personality characteristics may contribute to the fear of speaking, the tendency to remain silent or to avoid situations that may require talking is, in part, strengthened through experience. In the preceding chapters, we described the way in which your child may have developed this habit of avoiding feared situations by not talking. When your child is expected to talk, she feels anxious. Avoiding those situations, perhaps by avoiding eye contact or remaining silent, temporarily reduces the anxiety. The good news is that children with selective mutism can learn to speak without feeling so anxious. To help your child do this, we'll focus on those aspects of her surroundings that may be anxiety-provoking and discuss making some changes to the environment so your child feels more comfortable. Because selective mutism usually occurs at school, most parents will begin by working with their child's school staff members, focusing on the school setting. By implementing the strategies described in the following chapters, you'll help your child to feel more comfortable speaking in situations that are currently stressful for her.

PRINCIPLE TWO: SPEAKING IN GRADUAL STEPS HELPS FEAR GO AWAY

One way to overcome a fear is to face the anxiety-provoking situations one has avoided in the past. As noted in chapter 3, this strategy is called *exposure* and it's really a form of practice. In our work with children who have selective mutism and their families, we usually encourage parents and school personnel to gradually expose the child to feared speaking situations and ensure speaking at each step. This process involves first carefully identifying those aspects of situations that are anxiety-provoking. You can then create a hierarchy, or ladder, of feared situations, beginning with situations where your child currently talks comfortably, then moving to those where she talks less frequently, and ending with those where she does not talk at all.

In order to ensure your child's success at overcoming a fear of speaking, we'll start with the locations, people, and activities that currently lead your child to feel comfortable while speaking. In very small steps, your child's comfort with talking is gradually transferred from one successful situation to new situations by making changes to the people involved, the location, or the activity. For example, if your child will talk to you when reading in the school library, that ability to talk with confidence can then be transferred to another situation by making a small change to the scenario. Perhaps you could move your reading session, one small step at a time, to a busier part of the library or into another room in the school. As you can see, to help your child overcome selective mutism, it'll be important to identify the people your child speaks to, the locations in which your child speaks, and the activities that encourage your child to talk.

Climbing a conversational ladder is not unlike learning other skills. If you think back to when your child, or even you, learned to ride a bicycle, you probably recall how difficult and frightening that was at first. Yet through gradual steps, from first riding with someone holding onto the seat and handlebars, to riding with only the assistance of training wheels, and, finally, to riding unsupported without the training wheels, children learn to ride a bicycle. The key is to avoid the temptation to move too quickly up the ladder. Just as pushing a child to go down a hill on her first bicycle ride may not be the best way to help her learn, placing your child in situations that are too challenging too soon (and probably too anxiety-provoking) can cause your child to stop talking. You don't want that to happen! You want to be sure that your child will be successful talking in the new situation, even if she experiences some anxiety. To do that, you need to plan to transfer her confident speaking to new situations through small, manageable steps.

In chapter 7 you'll be taken through the step-by-step construction of your child's conversational ladder. In later chapters, we'll also present numerous suggestions based on these behavior principles to help you develop a comprehensive plan that will encourage your child to talk more frequently. For example, you will learn how to foster your child's talking at school through "conversational visits" in chapter 8, and how to improve peer connections between home and school through playdates in chapter 9.

PRINCIPLE THREE: TRACKING YOUR CHILD'S PROGRESS LETS YOU KNOW IF THE PLAN IS WORKING

We believe that a careful assessment of your child's difficulties is crucial to developing an intervention plan. So, in order to identify the most helpful strategies for your child's particular needs, the first step is to obtain a thorough understanding of your child's speaking patterns and comfort levels in a variety of situations. In chapter 3, we discussed the importance of gathering information about your child's speaking patterns and comfort levels with different people, locations, and activities. In chapters 6 and 7, you'll be encouraged to consider the ways in which your child's reactions differ depending on who is involved, where your child is, and what she is doing. It's important to be as specific as possible when detailing your child's reactions, because the better you understand the aspects of situations that provoke her anxiety, the better equipped you'll be to make helpful changes. By using the speaking situations assessment log provided in exercise 3.4, along with other monitoring forms presented in chapter 6, you will be able to systematically track the situations in which your child does and does not speak.

Once you start using the intervention strategies, you'll find it very helpful to continue tracking your child's talking and comfort levels in different situations, so you can monitor her progress. In all likelihood, your child will not begin talking comfortably in every situation overnight. Changes are often gradual and very subtle. Without careful monitoring, progress might be overlooked. These subtle differences in the situations where your child does and does not talk might also be useful when you're planning the next steps up your child's ladder toward speaking with greater confidence.

The information gathered through systematic tracking may also tell us about the effectiveness of the intervention. If the strategies are helpful, you can expect to see some changes in your child's comfort level when talking in different situations over a period of time. If you implement a particular strategy and then notice that your child is very uncomfortable or doesn't make any progress for some time, you need to consider making some changes to the intervention. Chapter 7 will describe when and how to make changes to the intervention plan.

PRINCIPLE FOUR: PRACTICE, PRACTICE, PRACTICE

We can't emphasize enough the importance of practice. As is the case with any new skill, practice is essential to overcoming the fear of speaking. As your child moves up the ladder, be sure to provide as many opportunities as possible for her to practice speaking. The more exposure or practice your child has at each step, the easier it will be for her to conquer the fear associated with that speaking situation. Learning to talk confidently in an increasing range of situations is hard work for the child with selective mutism. Incentives can sometimes help motivate a child to progress up the ladder; we'll talk more about that later in the book.

We also want to emphasize the need to maintain gains and to transfer successes to new situations. It's very important that you help to sustain the momentum, so that your child continues to move forward in speaking to a broader range of new people in different situations. In chapter 10, we offer some specific tips to expand your child's progress and sustain momentum.

PRINCIPLE FIVE: EARLY INTERVENTION IS BEST

Finally, the earlier you begin your child's intervention program, the better. Research suggests that treatment for selective mutism is more effective if it begins soon after the emergence of the mutism (Pionek Stone at al. 2002).

The chapter you've just finished reading has provided you with an overview of the five basic principles that guide our approach to intervention. If at any point in your reading of subsequent chapters you find that the rationale for a given strategy is unclear, we encourage you to come back to this chapter. If you and those helping your child can develop a solid understanding of these guiding principles, you'll be well armed when developing, monitoring, and making decisions about your child's intervention plan.

5

Setting Up the Management Team

CHAPTER OBJECTIVES

In this chapter you will learn the following:

- ★ What a management team is and why it is important

- ★ Whom to consider when choosing the management team

- ★ How to get the management team set up at the school

- ★ How often and when the management team should meet

- ★ How to keep records of management team meetings

By this point in the book, you've had a chance to learn about the characteristics of children with selective mutism, the reasons some children are afraid to speak, and the professionals who can help your child. In the last chapter, we introduced the basic principles of the program presented in this book. Now, let's get started discussing the ways in which you, and the professionals you work with, can help your child overcome selective mutism.

WHAT IS A MANAGEMENT TEAM AND WHY IS IT IMPORTANT?

Helping your child overcome selective mutism requires the efforts of many adults from your child's world, including you, supportive family and friends, and professionals. For this reason, the first step in developing an intervention plan is to put together a team of individuals who will collaborate with you and each other and are committed to helping your child. We call this group of people your child's "management team."

As we've described earlier in the book, your child's selective mutism is likely to be most apparent at school. You may notice that your child talks comfortably only at home. Or your child may talk without trouble at home and in the community, yet not at school. Regardless of the extent of your child's mutism, it's likely that he feels less comfortable talking within the school setting. So, it makes sense to recruit school staff to join you in helping your child.

Based on our clinical experience, we know that working through selective mutism takes time and patience. A slow yet systematic approach, with regular monitoring of progress and careful planning of the next steps, works best. If several individuals work as a team to support your child, the intervention will benefit from the observations and good ideas of all team members. As you can imagine, brainstorming and problem solving are more productive with several people participating in the process!

WHO SHOULD JOIN YOUR MANAGEMENT TEAM?

The successful management of selective mutism requires cooperation between parents, the classroom teacher(s), school administrators, and other professionals. Depending on staffing at your child's school and the availability of other professionals, your child's management team will be unique in its composition. In the case of Jason, a seven-year-old in second grade, the management team included his mother, grandmother (who provided after-school care), the classroom teacher, the gym teacher, and the school principal. For Karen, a six-year-old in kindergarten, the management team consisted of both parents (although her father is the one who attends most of the meetings given his more flexible work schedule), the classroom teacher, the school's special education teacher, and Karen's day-care provider. A psychologist from the school board with expertise in behavioral approaches provided consultation to the team, as needed.

As you can see, there's no one formula for composing a management team. To help you decide whom to involve, below we've listed some of the people you should consider.

Parent(s) or Guardian(s)

At least one parent or guardian should attend all meetings of the management team. As a parent or guardian, you have important contributions to make to both the initial assessment of your child's selective mutism and its management. You know your child's abilities better than anyone. In fact, as a parent, you'll need to take on most of the responsibility of helping your child overcome selective mutism. The fact that you're reading this book shows your commitment to helping your child. Although it's critical to have the input of school staff members and available professionals, you'll be the one working with your child through the day-to-day steps of the intervention. Given your central role on the management team, it's important that you're knowledgeable about selective mutism, understand the basic principles of the intervention plan, and are available to work with school staff to ensure your child gets the help that he needs.

Principal

Because the management of your child's selective mutism will take place primarily at school, it's important to invite the principal or school administrator to join the management team. As the head administrator at the school, the principal needs to be aware of your child's special needs and support the efforts of the management team to help your child overcome selective mutism. The principal or administrator will probably need to approve of any classroom modifications that are made to ensure that your child's fear of speaking doesn't interfere with his academic progress. If a teacher has difficulty evaluating your child's academic abilities in conventional ways, alternative methods may need to be approved by the principal. (We'll discuss teacher evaluation issues more closely in an upcoming chapter.)

The school principal may also be very helpful when it comes to practical issues. In chapter 8, we'll describe how parent conversational visits to the school can be beneficial to your child. The school principal may be useful in deciding what room can be made available to you and letting you know the best times to visit the school for these special meetings. The school principal's participation is particularly important during the management team's initial planning sessions.

Teachers

One of the primary goals of the intervention will be to help your child become more comfortable speaking in the classroom. The teacher will be an important ally of yours as you work to achieve this goal. Your child's teacher will need to understand selective mutism and be willing to modify interactions with your child, seat him in a location that will encourage talking with classmates, design classroom activities that allow your child to participate nonverbally when necessary, and consider whether alternative evaluation approaches would be helpful. The classroom teacher will also be the member of the management team who can share daily observations of your child's progress within the classroom.

Your child might also have regular interactions with other instructors, such as the gym, music, or art teacher. If your child is older and has a rotating class schedule, several teachers might be involved. At minimum, try to have at least one regular classroom teacher involved. For older children, that might be the homeroom teacher or the teacher who sees your child most regularly. If other teachers are able to participate in the management team, their involvement will help the team transfer the intervention strategies to different classes and track your child's progress across settings.

When considering teachers who might join the management team, you'll want to find out whether your child's school has a staff member who oversees programming for children with special learning needs. Depending on the school system, this person might be called a "special-education" or "resource" teacher. Although your child may not have learning difficulties per se, a special-education teacher's experience with finding creative ways to meet children's needs within the school environment can be a wonderful asset to the management team. Because your child may still benefit from supports during the next school year, a specialized teacher like this can often remain involved with the management team from one year to the next. This continuity is critical, since it ensures that at least one school staff person on the team remains constant over time.

Expert Consultants

Since many parents, teachers, and principals may be unfamiliar with selective mutism, it's important to recruit a professional from the community who is more knowledgeable about this problem. Successful interventions for children with selective mutism also require knowledge of typical child development, academic skills development, and the behavioral principles that support the intervention strategies to be used. Psychologists and those with a background in psychology often have knowledge in these areas and can provide guidance to the management team. Professionals from other backgrounds (such as speech-language pathologists or family physicians) may also be appropriate choices for your team, depending on their training and/or interest in learning about selective mutism. With the help of school staff members, you might be able to identify a professional from the school board staff who would be an asset to the team, such as a social worker with expertise in working with anxious children, or a behavior management consultant. In an ideal situation, the expert consultant would attend all management team meetings. However, if this type of time commitment is impossible, work with your expert consultant to ensure regular, though less frequent, participation.

Management Team Facilitator

Coordinating regularly scheduled team meetings is a critical job. It will be important for you to be available for all meetings and for school staff to attend meetings over the course of the school year. To help coordinate school staff members' schedules so that the entire team can attend meetings, you might look to a school-based team facilitator for assistance. This person can also ensure active participation from all team members, keep the group on task during planning sessions, and take the lead in any problem-solving sessions. The management team facilitator may be an additional member of your team, or you may find that someone already on the team would work well in that role. For instance, the school principal, classroom teacher, or special-education teacher might be a suitable candidate for the job.

Exercise 5.1   Composing Your Child's Management Team

Take out your notebook or journal and write down information on those you would like to invite to participate as members of the management team. Using the sample table below as a guide, make one column to list team members' names, another to list their titles and possible roles on the team, and another to jot down their phone numbers and other contact information. Be sure to list yourself, the classroom teacher, and any other school staff members who could take part in helping your child. Have you missed anyone on your recruitment list?

Team member's name	Title/role in team	Phone number
Jane	Mother	834-7754
Ms. Taylor	Classroom teacher Team facilitator	721-8634
Mr. Philips	Principal School contact person	721-8646

| Regina Hernandez | Behavior management consultant (staff member) | 835-5461 |
| Timothy Andrews | Speech-language pathologist (staff member) | 722-8759 |

HOW DO YOU SET UP THE MANAGEMENT TEAM?

Now that you've identified people who could contribute to the management team, it's important for you to share this information with school staff members on the list of possible team members. If school staff have previously been involved in assisting your child, you may already have a team set up or have an idea about who would be able to help organize the team. If you have yet to be in contact with school staff about intervention planning for your child, you need to make the necessary arrangements as soon as possible.

As a parent, you might be feeling unsure about how to get the intervention set up at the school, and uncomfortable approaching school staff. Remember, it's not uncommon for children with selective mutism to have parents who also tend to be shy and less comfortable talking with others. But we encourage you to take on the role of advocate for your child by asking for help from the people who work at his school. In reading this book, you are learning a great deal about selective mutism and strategies that will be helpful to your child. The teachers at your child's school may be less familiar with this relatively uncommon problem but would likely be interested in finding out ways to help. In our experience, despite the fact that the available staff members can vary from one school to another, there's always a desire to make things better for your child.

Although the organizational structure of every school is different, it's often a good idea to start by making an appointment with the school principal. During that meeting, you can talk about your concerns for your child (if the principal isn't already aware of them), offer to share information from this book, and ask for input regarding good candidates for the management team. Because the principal oversees all activities within the school, he or she may volunteer to help set up the management team and arrange the first meeting. Alternatively, the principal may direct you to another staff person who could take on the role of management team facilitator. Either way, you'll be building an important working relationship at the school, where much of the work to help your child needs to take place. You'll also be letting the principal know that you want to do your part to help with the intervention program.

Exercise 5.2   Contacting the School

If you haven't yet had regular contact with the school regarding your child's selective mutism, contact the principal or another appropriate high-level staff member to arrange an initial meeting. You might want to let him or her know that the purpose of the meeting is to talk about your interest in developing an intervention program for your child and that you hope the school's staff will be able to assist you. In preparation for that meeting, take out your notebook or journal and make a list of the things that you would like to discuss with the principal. Some of the questions you might want to ask include the following:

Is the school principal (and his or her staff) familiar with selective mutism and ways to help children overcome a fear of speaking?

Is the principal open to setting up a school-based intervention program?

Is the principal available to help you set up a management team, or could that task be assigned to a staff member?

Can the principal make any suggestions regarding other professionals from the school board who might be able to serve as expert consultants to the team?

Keep in mind that principals have very busy schedules, so you'll want to make the best use of his or her time. The more prepared you are for the meeting, the more productive and successful the meeting will be!

HOW OFTEN AND WHERE SHOULD THE MANAGEMENT TEAM MEET?

A successful intervention program requires regular meetings of the management team. At each meeting, the management team will review progress, resolve problems, and plan the next steps in the intervention program. Where possible, efforts should be made to include all members of the management team at each meeting. Given the busy schedules of school staff, however, there may be times when some members may not be able to attend. We recommend that you and the team facilitator be present at all meetings. The team facilitator can act as a liaison with absent school staffers by gathering relevant information prior to the meeting and sharing the outcome of the meeting with team members who are unable to attend.

The Frequency of Meetings

During the initial stages of the intervention, a lot of planning and adjustments to the program will be necessary. During this time, meetings might be scheduled more frequently. For example, Jason's management team planned to meet two times a month and Karen's team was able to meet four times a month at the beginning. Once the intervention is in place and your child is making steady progress, meetings might be scheduled less frequently, such as once a month. When logistical issues result in a missed monthly meeting, periodic phone calls between you and the facilitator help keep the intervention on track. Checking in like this can help you solve problems that have come up, make adjustments to the program, and support the efforts of the team when progress is slower.

Location of Team Meetings

It's recommended that the management team meetings take place at the school. In addition to the practical benefits for participating school staff, the school setting can inspire ideas during planning sessions. If possible, conduct team meetings in your child's actual classroom. By meeting in the space where your child spends most of his time (and likely feels most reluctant to talk), management team members will be able to develop an appreciation of your child's daily experiences. Being aware of the layout of the room, where the teacher and students sit, and the activities available to students can spur creativity when planning and adjusting the intervention program. This also makes it easy for members of the management team to view samples of your child's class work (for example, drawings, writing samples, or math assignments) and to appreciate your child's academic abilities.

Exercise 5.3   Scheduling Regular Team Meetings

At your first management team meeting, bring along your journal or notebook and your own calendar. With the team, think about possible times to meet and how often everyone is available. During the initial planning stages and when your child is making rapid progress, remember that it will be helpful to meet at least two times per month. Thereafter, monthly meetings will likely work well. What time of day works best for team members? Often, school staff members find it easiest to meet in the morning before class begins, during the lunch hour, or immediately after school. Can you arrange your own schedule to be available at such times? If at all possible, try to accommodate the preferences of school staff. Try to schedule a couple of months' worth of meetings in advance (such as every other Monday afternoon at 3:30 P.M. for two months), so that everyone can block out time to meet on a regular basis. In your notebook or journal, write down the date, time, and location of all meeting times scheduled for intervention planning.

6

What Comes First in the Intervention?

CHAPTER OBJECTIVES

In this chapter you will learn the following:

★ How to make school a positive experience for your child

★ How changes to your child's seating position in the classroom can increase the likelihood of speaking (and decrease anxiety) during the school day

★ How you can assess your child's comfort level (and anxiety level) about school

★ How the teacher can assess your child's comfort level (and anxiety level) at school

---

MAKING THE SCHOOL EXPERIENCE POSITIVE FOR YOUR CHILD

With your management team now organized, you're ready to begin planning the initial steps of the school-based intervention for your child. Before introducing your child to her conversational ladder and assisting her to gradually climb it, there are some things you can do to prepare her. Given that much of the work will take place at school, the very place your child probably has the most difficulty, you want to ensure that she's feeling as positive and relaxed as possible about school in general. Below we suggest ways that you and the rest of the management team can help your child feel comfortable and positive about her school experiences.

Encourage Participation in School Activities

Despite the fact that your child may not be comfortable speaking in certain school situations (or other places) right now, you and the management team need to encourage your child to participate at least nonverbally wherever possible. That means your child should be encouraged and expected to participate fully in all classroom activities through nonverbal means. Teachers might invite your child to be responsible for classroom chores that don't require speaking. For example, Christopher, a second-grader, was asked to pass out books and papers to classmates at the beginning of lessons. Jessica, a third-grade student, was asked to write the date on the blackboard each day and on occasion served as a messenger by taking notes from the teacher to the office.

Your child also should be encouraged to participate in extracurricular activities where possible. For example, Christopher took a nonspeaking role in the school play, and Jessica joined a sports team. By participating in after-school activities (even if only nonverbally for now), your child will be showing classmates and teachers some of her true abilities. Increased participation in school activities, even if it doesn't involve speaking, can lead to a sense of accomplishment, greater self-confidence, and higher self-esteem. These are important experiences for your child, and they're often necessary first steps on the conversational ladder toward speaking comfortably and confidently.

Exercise 6.1   Encouraging Participation at School

With the help of your management team, brainstorm about any school-based activities your child could participate in without being required to speak. Think about responsibilities your child could assume in the classroom, as well as more-structured extracurricular activities offered at the school. Record your ideas in your notebook or journal, identifying the activities she could start right away and those that could be introduced later, as in the sample chart below.

	Activities that allow nonverbal participation	When?
1.	Classroom: hands out materials to fellow students	Now; every day
2.	Classroom: brings teacher's messages to the office	Now; occasionally
3.	Schoolwide: intramural volleyball	Winter term

Remember, the purpose is to provide your child with positive experiences at school that do not require speaking, but not to overwhelm your child with too many new expectations all at once.

Encourage Participation in Community Activities

As a parent, you can also encourage your child to participate nonverbally in extracurricular activities in the community. You might enroll her in a sports team, a dance class, or music lessons. Regardless of whether she feels comfortable speaking to her instructor or classmates, extracurricular activities can provide your child the opportunity to develop new skills and experience a sense of mastery. Extracurricular activities in the community also provide an opportunity for your child to interact with peers in a setting where she may feel more comfortable speaking—away from school. Children with selective mutism often first become comfortable speaking with peers in the community before they will speak with peers in the school.

Exercise 6.2 Planning Extracurricular Activities in the Community

In your notebook or journal, make a list of extracurricular activities your child is currently involved in and those she has enjoyed in the

past. Add to the list other activities that your child has indicated interest in or those you think would be a good match to her current
interests. Are these activities that she could participate in without
speaking? Also, think about the children she might interact with during each activity. Are any children from her school or classroom also
enrolled?

When you've made your list, see if you can identify the activities that your child would enjoy, those she could comfortably participate in without speaking, and those that would allow her
opportunities to spend time with schoolmates. Remember, your
child is likely to first speak with a classmate outside of the school
setting before she'll talk with that same peer at school. Seeing other
children from her class through extracurricular activities on a regular basis can be a great way for her to become more comfortable
interacting with schoolmates.

The example below shows the ideas that Jessica's parents came
up with as possible extracurricular activities for their daughter.
Jessica's parents circled Girl Scouts as the best opportunity for their
daughter to interact with classmates outside of the school setting.

	Extracurricular activity	Can my child participate nonverbally?	Are any schoolmates or classmates also participating?
1.	Swimming lessons	Yes	No
2.	Soccer	Yes	Yes—student from school who's one year older
3.	Girl Scouts	Yes	Yes—two classmates

Take the Pressure Off

It's important to avoid placing undue pressure on your child to
speak. Parents and teachers alike should not make speaking demands

the child will inevitably fail to meet. For example, it wouldn't be help-ful for a teacher to ask Jessica to answer questions in front of the class when she's not comfortable even whispering to her seatmate. As a parent, you too should avoid the temptation to convince your child to speak by asking her to use her words in a circumstance she's not ready to face.

Likewise, offering rewards or punishments won't encourage your child to speak if she's not ready. Have you ever found yourself offer-ing to give your child a treat just so she would finally speak to that distant relative at a family function? Maybe you've been so desperate to help your child start speaking that you've told her she may lose certain privileges if she doesn't make progress. Perhaps a teacher has offered your child bonus marks on a project if she would just say a few words about it. In the case of Christopher, for example, his teacher thought he'd be enticed to speak if he had to talk directly to the teacher in order to sign up for pizza day. Incentives such as these can sometimes be powerful motivators for children, if they are well timed and appropriate to the circumstances. However, offers of incentives can actually slow progress or make your child more anxious about speaking if they are introduced at the wrong time and in the wrong way.

We completely understand why the adults who care about your child might be eager to nudge her to face her fear. It's only natural for people to hope that, with the right motivator, she will get past this problem more quickly. If only it were that simple. Pressure, offers of rewards, negative consequences for not speaking, and attempts to sur-prise your child into speaking can become sources of tremendous anx-iety and may compound the problem. Unsuccessful efforts to pressure a child to speak only increase anxiety, cause the child to associate anxiety with the situation (for example, the other people present), and can even make your child's fear of speaking worse.

Pressure-to-speak scenarios, camouflaged as incentives, also become situations that your child may try to avoid. Each time she avoids a pressure situation, she feels relief at not experiencing the anticipated anxiety. This type of avoidance behavior is reinforced and she may actually become less likely to face speaking situations tied to incentives. Has your child ever been successfully enticed to speak by an offer of a reward? Or have you found that she avoids situations completely that are associated with incentives? Later in this book, we'll describe how incentives can in fact be a very important part of the intervention when your child has moved to more challenging steps on the conversational ladder. But their usage must be carefully planned to occur at a time when they will serve as a motivator and not simply as a source of pressure.

Even if you don't use overt incentives, try to be aware of more subtle ways you might be inadvertently pressuring your child to speak. We often hear from well-intentioned parents that they may ask their child, at the end of the school day, if they spoke to any classmates or teachers that day. While this is important information for you to have as a parent, making this a focus of after-school conversation with your child may be interpreted as added pressure. It's our experience that, in general, children with selective mutism want to feel comfortable speaking at school—they want to be able to answer by saying "Yes, I did!" But, in reality, your child may need to take many steps before she can get to that point. As an alternative, why not seek out progress reports from other members of the management team or other adults who may observe your child in settings where she typically does not speak. The bottom line is this: You and other adults working with your child need to be careful not to pressure her about speaking. Pressures to speak, regardless of how well-intentioned, could compound your child's fear of speaking.

CLASSROOM SEATING ARRANGEMENTS

Adjusting your child's seating arrangement in the classroom can be a simple-to-implement strategy that can increase your child's general comfort level and decrease speaking-related anxiety during the school day. Children with selective mutism often move more quickly up the steps toward confident speaking when they have opportunities for informal interactions with other students. During early phases of the intervention, interactions with peers may be nonverbal. But over time, these nonverbal interactions help to establish relationships with peers that will naturally lead to speaking. Your child's seating location relative to nearby classmates and the general structure of the classroom can significantly affect your child's general comfort level, increase opportunities that require peer interaction, and ultimately lead to speaking.

Work with the classroom teacher to select the best seating location for your child. The following is a discussion of what you should consider when making that selection.

Choice of Seatmate(s)

If your child is in the first grade or higher, it's likely that much of her day is spent at a desk in the classroom. Depending on the classroom teacher's seating layout, your child may be seated by herself as part of a row of desks or perhaps in a small grouping of desks. Regardless of the classroom layout, it's beneficial to seat your child next to students she prefers. Remember, particularly in the beginning phases of the intervention, you want your child to build friendships and become comfortable interacting with classmates at school. If she is not interested in her assigned seatmate, she'll be less likely to share common interests or be drawn into nonverbal interactions and conversations with that child. Good candidates for seatmates include peers your child is comfortable with, speaks fondly of during after-school conversations, or identifies as her friends.

Most important, consider whether there are any children in the class who your child already speaks to, either at school or in the community. For example Olivia, a seven-year-old in second grade, attends a swimming class at a local recreation center with one of her school classmates, Lisa. Although Olivia has yet to speak to any of her peers at school, Olivia's mother has observed her whispering and giggling with this classmate during swimming lessons. Recently, Olivia has even asked if this friend could come over to the house to play sometime. Olivia's swimming-class friend would make a great choice as a seatmate at school. Ben, a nine-year-old in fourth grade, is already speaking to a select few classmates while on the playground at recess, and he's been known to whisper to one boy in particular during physical education class in the gym. What do you think might happen if that boy were seated next to Ben in class, instead of the two girls he's currently seated with?

Location of Your Child's Seat in the Classroom

We've talked about how physical location can have an impact on your child's general comfort level (or anxiety level) and the likelihood that she will speak in a given situation. During the regular routines of the classroom, those same principles regarding physical location apply. For example, your child is more likely to first speak to peers in places that are more private and make her feel more relaxed and less anxious.

SEATING AT THE BACK OF THE CLASS

You may be able to increase your child's feeling of privacy and decrease anxiety by moving her to a seat near the back of the class-room, behind most other students. A seating location of this kind may allow her to speak to one child without being seen or heard by other children in the class. By increasing your child's privacy, she'll be less likely to be noticed by her classmates and therefore less likely to become the center of attention for speaking in situations where she usually doesn't speak. We've heard many stories of how an enthusias-tic classmate announced it to the class the first time the child with selective mutism was observed speaking to someone. Although these declarations may be well-intentioned and are difficult to avoid entirely, it's helpful to decrease their likelihood as your child makes those first steps toward overcoming her selective mutism. The antici-pated reactions of others can become another source of anxiety and perceived pressure for your child, so it's best to seat her in a location where she's not being observed by the whole class.

SEATING AWAY FROM THE CLASSROOM EXIT

Ensuring that your child has an opportunity to interact with peers more privately might also require assessing your child's seating location in relation to the classroom door. Many teachers leave the classroom door open for at least a portion of the school day. But even if classroom instruction takes place behind closed doors, recess time, lunch time, and packing up for the day result in lots of traffic past desks near the classroom exit; if your child's seat is near the door, her privacy and general comfort level are likely reduced by classroom traffic, hallway traffic, and the perceived risk of onlookers. Are there other seating locations in the classroom that could offer your child more privacy during the busy parts of the day?

SEATING AWAY FROM THE CLASSROOM TEACHER

When determining the best location for your child's seat in the class, you and your management team should also take into consideration the typical location of the classroom teacher. If your child feels more comfortable with classmates than with the teacher, this is particularly important. Seating your child at a distance from the classroom teacher's desk or place where he or she typically teaches (for example, the blackboard) may reduce anxiety and increase the likelihood of spontaneous conversation with a peer. On the other hand, if your child feels more comfortable in the presence of adults than children at school, it might be important to seat her near the classroom teacher.

Similarly, if your child has special learning needs, it may be more important that she be located near the front of the room in order to better see the blackboard or be near the teacher's desk for remedial assistance. Your child's seating location is best determined in collaboration with the classroom teacher, who has the best understanding of your child's learning needs and her preference for peer or adult interaction.

ORIENTATION OF DESKS

In addition to looking at the location of your child's desk in the classroom, it's also helpful to consider the actual orientation of the desks. This point will be most relevant if your child spends her day in a group seating arrangement, rather than in a single desk facing the front of the room. We've discovered that children with selective mutism tend to be most comfortable first speaking to others when they're not directly facing their conversational partner. Why do you think that might be? Our guess is that a child may find it easier to speak to someone when she's not making eye contact. Remember, we believe that children with selective mutism experience a specific fear of being heard or *seen* speaking. In essence, by speaking to someone who is not directly facing her, she can be heard but not seen. This may be a somewhat less-anxiety-provoking way for the child to first speak in a new situation.

For children seated in grouped desks, we typically recommend that the peer your child is most likely to speak with be seated beside her. At first, your child will be much more likely to lean over and whisper into her neighbor's ear than speak to that same classmate from across the desk. Once your child feels comfortable speaking with the classmate seated next to her, it may be helpful to move that trusted conversational partner across the table and assign a new peer to the desk beside her.

Exercise 6.3 Applying What You've Learned About Seating Arrangements

As a way to get you thinking about how seating arrangements can affect your child's comfort level when she's speaking, let's apply the general principles you've just learned. As you may recall, Olivia is a seven-year-old in second grade who does well academically and is liked by her peers. To date, Olivia has not yet felt comfortable speaking to any children or adults at the school. Her teacher, Ms. Bell, often uses the blackboard at the front of the room and tends to sit at her desk while the students do seat work. Below, you'll see a diagram of the classroom's layout.

Notice that Olivia's classroom teacher has placed students' desks in groups of four, with the students facing each other. What else do you notice about where Olivia's desk is located? Think about the compatibility of seatmates, the location of her desk relative to the teacher and the classroom exit, and, most important, the privacy factor. Can you think of some other options for Olivia's seating that might put her more at ease and encourage opportunities for her to speak with others? Take out your notebook or journal and jot down your ideas. Compare your suggestions to the plan developed by Olivia's management team.

Clearly, there are many options, but here are some of the things her team considered when they were making their selections:

- Olivia might be more likely to first speak in the classroom if she were seated next to her friend Lisa, who's in her swimming class and whom she already whispers to in other settings. To

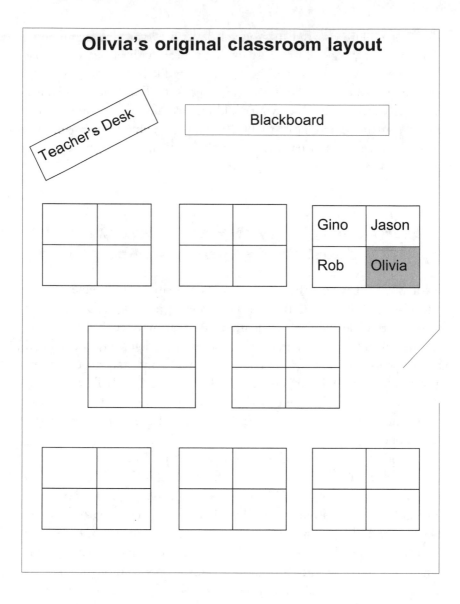

Olivia's original classroom layout

Teacher's Desk

Blackboard

Gino	Jason
Rob	Olivia

begin, the team decided that this student should be seated next to Olivia. Once Olivia became comfortable speaking to Lisa in the classroom, she could be moved across the desk from Olivia and another peer could be seated directly next to her.

■ In the original seating arrangement, Olivia was seated at the front of the room, where even whispers to her neighbor could be viewed by the rest of the class. As an alternative, the

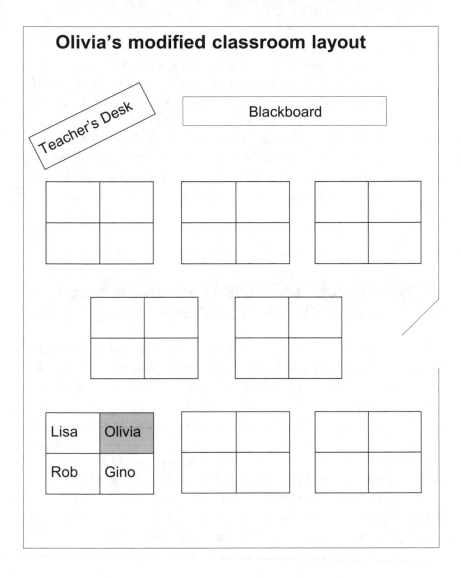

management team suggested that Olivia be seated at the very back of the classroom with her back to the teacher.

■ Olivia was originally seated close to the classroom exit and the hallway. The management team suggested that she'd feel more comfortable if seated on the opposite side of the classroom. Again, as a result, Olivia's privacy would be improved and student traffic would be less likely to interrupt her speaking opportunities.

■ Ms. Bell typically taught from the front of the room and often worked at her desk while students were involved in seat work. Given the fact that Olivia was a strong student without any particular learning difficulties, the team suggested that she might feel more comfortable and relaxed at a distance from the classroom teacher. Although Olivia quite likes her teacher and Ms. Bell is a warm and friendly person, Olivia's anxiety regarding speaking at school was likely to be heightened in the teacher's presence.

Were your ideas similar to ours?

Exercise 6.4 Identifying an Optimal Seating Arrangement for Your Child

Now that you've had a chance to think about how seating arrangements can increase opportunities for a child to feel more comfortable interacting and possibly speaking, it's time to think about your own child. Take out your notebook or journal. If you're unfamiliar with the layout of your child's classroom, make a list of questions you can ask the teacher about her seating arrangement. For instance, where is your child's seat located in the room? Who sits near her? Where does the teacher typically spend most of his or her time within the classroom? If you already have the answers to these types of questions, assess your child's current seating arrangement. Does it provide her with the most privacy for speaking to peers? Can you think of seating locations in the room that might maximize your child's comfort level for speaking with others?

Discuss your child's current seating location with your child's management team, and the classroom teacher in particular. If other seating locations are more optimal, would the classroom teacher be willing to move your child's assigned seat? In planning a change in seating, be sure to consider any other learning needs. Finally, remember that the management team will need to monitor the benefits of your child's seating assignment. Modifications to your child's seating arrangement may be helpful as the school year progresses and your child becomes more comfortable speaking at school.

ASSESSING YOUR CHILD'S COMFORT LEVELS AT SCHOOL

As your child participates more fully at school and undue pressures to speak are removed, she is likely to become more relaxed in the school setting. You may find that your child seems to be enjoying school more. For example, Jessica's mother noticed that she seemed more eager to get to school each day and sometimes talked excitedly about things she was learning in class. Teachers also may notice that your child is participating more in daily activities and that her nonverbal communication (for example, pointing and other gesturing) has increased in the classroom. Christopher's teacher noticed that he was interacting a lot more with the children seated near him, often smiling and pointing at things to express himself. Observations of this kind can indicate that your child's general comfort level has increased and that anxiety tied to the school setting has been reduced. Children with selective mutism need to feel secure and comfortable in their surroundings before they will speak in places they haven't before.

Changes in your child's comfort levels are important markers of progress, but they can be so subtle that you may not easily notice them. At least in the beginning stages of the intervention program, carefully keep track of your child's observed comfort levels in various school-related situations. You can think of your child's *comfort level* as the degree to which she experiences a situation without anxiety. Although it's impossible for you to know what it's like for your child when she's anxious, you can probably learn a lot by looking closely at her behavior. When your child is anxious, she may appear more withdrawn, physically tense, and inhibited. The more comfortable your child is, the less likely it is that she will seem anxious or avoidant. Both you and your child's teacher can assess comfort levels by observing your child in daily activities at school.

Exercise 6.5   Assessing Your Child's Comfort Levels in Daily Activities

1. Take out your notebook or journal and set up a log to record your estimates of your child's comfort levels in various school-

related situations. First, make a list of school-related scenarios in which you observe your child regularly. You might include activities like getting ready for school in the morning, leaving for school, arriving at the playground, or doing homework. Then, beside each activity, make a space to record how comfortable (as opposed to anxious) your child seems in that activity. We suggest you use a scale to indicate relative comfort in each activity. Your log could look something like the one that follows on page 79.

2. At least at the beginning of the program, we suggest that you fill out the log once a week. If one of the activities didn't occur during that time, you can estimate how your child would have responded given your other observations. Many parents find this to be a very helpful way to tune into their child's daily school-related anxiety levels. Some parents also find a form like this to be useful as a means to track how changes in school routines (for example, adjusting to a new teacher, or transitioning back to school after a vacation) affect their child's general anxiety levels. Remember that many children with selective mutism have temperaments that make changes in routine more difficult and potential sources of anxiety. Does your child seem to have more difficulty adjusting to changes in routines? Have you noticed that she becomes more reluctant about school at such times?

Systematic records of your observations can be shared with the members of your management team during regular meetings. Although teachers and other staff members might have a sense of your child's comfort levels while she's at school, it's helpful for them to also be aware of how she reacts to school-related activities outside of the school setting. Depending on the extent of your child's mutism, you may choose to use this type of log throughout the intervention or instead limit usage to critical periods. For instance, Christopher's mother knew that her son had a lot of trouble facing the school day and that it would be important to track subtle changes in his comfort levels around school each week. Jessica's parents, on the other hand, have always found her to be positive about school despite her trouble with speaking to the teacher. So Jessica's parents used the log at the beginning of the program and then again at times of significant changes to her daily routines (for example, returning to school after a vacation or an illness) or the intervention plan.

Comfort level in daily activities: Parent's log

	Extremely anxious	Very anxious	Anxious	Neutral	Comfortable	Very comfortable
Getting up on school mornings						
Getting dressed for school						
Breakfast on school mornings						
Leaving for school						
Arriving on playground						
Going into class						
Returning home from school						
Doing homework						
Talking with parent about school day						
Getting ready for bed						

Comfort level in daily activities: Teacher's log

	Extremely anxious	Very anxious	Anxious	Neutral	Comfortable	Very comfortable
Completing work silently at desk (e.g., math or silent reading)						
Completing nonspeaking task in front of class (for example, updating calendar, pointing to weather chart)						
Giving show-and-tell presentation or doing other speaking activity in front of class						
Responding to teacher's question that does not require a verbal response (e.g., pointing)						
Doing small-group activities with other children (e.g., crafts)						
Speaking to other children in classroom						
Being *observed* by others while speaking (e.g., peers observe child speaking; teacher observes him/her speaking with peers)						
Being *heard* by others while speaking (e.g., peers overhear child speaking to parents at school; teacher overhears child talking to peer)						
Playing with other children at recess						
Lunch						
Getting ready to go home						

Exercise 6.6   Teacher Observations of Your Child's Comfort Levels

1. At your next management team meeting, work with your team to create a similar log that the teacher can use to record your child's comfort levels in situations at school. First, make a list of school-based scenarios in which the teacher observes your child regularly. Try to include both nonverbal and verbal situations in the classroom and in other locations at school. Depending on your child's grade level and her classroom routines, the teacher's log will be unique to your child's daily school experiences.

2. Next, make a space for the teacher to record how comfortable (as opposed to anxious) your child seems in each activity. For comparison purposes, it's helpful if the teacher uses the same scale you developed for the parent version of the log, in exercise 6.5. After the team has decided on what should be included on the log, create a final draft for teaching staff to use. The teacher's log for tracking your child's comfort levels could look something like the one that follows.

    Given the fact that your child is probably less comfortable at school than at home, it's likely that your team can easily generate a list of school-related activities that might reveal something about your child's current comfort levels.

3. Ask the classroom teacher to fill out the log once a week. If one of the activities didn't occur during that time, the teacher can give an estimate of your child's comfort level in that situation based on other observations. Here's a tip: Some teachers find it helpful to seek out the observations of other staff who may see your child regularly at school (for example, the gym teacher or lunchroom monitor). If your child is older and on a rotating class schedule, several teachers can be invited to fill out the log as a means to gauge relative comfort levels in different class settings.

    Whereas your home-based observations of your child's comfort levels may be helpful in the early stages of the intervention, the teacher's log can provide ongoing information about your child's progress throughout the intervention program. Because progress can be subtle and your child is unlikely to begin talking comfortably in all situations at once, ongoing assessment of her comfort and anxiety levels over time can be an important way to monitor progress.

7

How Do You Set Up Your Child's Conversational Ladder?

CHAPTER OBJECTIVES

In this chapter you will do the following:

★ Review the importance of activities, locations, and people as factors that affect your child's comfort level in various speaking situations

★ Learn how to create a separate ladder for each factor—activities, locations, and people—and how to decide what steps should come first on each ladder

★ Construct a complete, integrated ladder for speaking at school by combining the activity, location, and people ladders

In chapter 3, we introduced the notion of exposure as a way for an individual to learn to face his fear. Instead of avoiding fearful experiences, a person exposes himself to the situations that make him somewhat anxious or uncomfortable. With practice, a person typically comes to be less anxious when later placed in the same circumstance. Exposure is a powerful tool for working through fears of all sorts, and it can be very helpful for children working through a fear of speaking. As we described in chapter 4, gradual exposure is an important part of the program, which you'll learn about in this chapter. In very small steps, your child can be provided opportunities to practice talking in increasingly challenging situations. By moving step-by-step through a carefully planned sequence of situations, your child can gradually transfer to new situations his newly acquired confidence in speaking. Think back to chapter 1, where you read about the gradual stages that children with selective mutism typically move through when working toward feeling comfortable about talking at school. You can think of these stages as general steps on your child's conversational ladder.

So, how do you identify ladder steps that will be suited to your child? As you've read earlier in this book, there are often common characteristics among children with this difficulty. However, remember that each child with selective mutism is an individual. For this reason, the conversational ladder will need to be tailored to the specifics of your child's own fear of speaking.

To develop a conversational ladder that your child can successfully climb, you'll need to be creative and plan carefully. In order to build a ladder that will work for your child, you'll need to work with your management team to do the initial planning. This should be an important focus of upcoming team meetings. It's often very helpful to brainstorm with others about possible practice situations or potential steps on your child's conversational ladder. School personnel will be particularly helpful in identifying practice opportunities at school— the setting where your child probably has the most trouble speaking comfortably.

REVISITING THE INFLUENCE OF ACTIVITIES, LOCATIONS, AND PEOPLE

In chapter 2, we talked about how your child's speaking patterns likely vary depending on the circumstances. You're probably aware that your child talks with ease in some situations yet becomes quite nervous or even unable to talk in others. The question you might ask yourself is, Why are there differences? In our experience, we've found that three factors tend to determine whether a child with selective mutism will be more or less comfortable speaking in a given situation: the people present, the physical location or setting, and the activity occurring at that moment. These three factors can vary within any situation that requires speaking. For instance, you might find that your child is surprisingly quiet when a classmate comes over for a playdate (people factor), despite the fact that he's at home (location factor) and playing games that he typically enjoys (activity factor). Similarly, you might find that your child becomes increasingly quiet while talking to you (people factor) on your walk (activity factor) to school (location factor) in the morning. Regardless of the speaking situation, it's likely that each factor contributes to some extent to your child's relative comfort level in using his words to communicate. By identifying speaking-related opportunities in which each factor varies, you and your management team can build a conversational ladder that'll help your child get over the wall of anxiety that prevents him from speaking at school.

GETTING STARTED BUILDING A CONVERSATIONAL LADDER

Given the fact that the school is probably the place where your child experiences the most anxiety when talking, this chapter will focus on helping you construct a ladder for getting over a fear of speaking at school. In chapter 8, you'll learn about how you and your management team can help your child climb up the conversational ladder for school. In chapter 9, you'll learn how you can build a conversational ladder to help your child overcome a fear of speaking in other situations, like playdates or extracurricular activities in the community.

Okay, let's get started. In the pages to follow, you'll be walked through a series of exercises that will help you identify steps on your child's ladder for speaking at school. Although you should finalize the school-based ladder with the management team, you'll need to do some of your own thinking, given what you know about your child. To complete the following exercises, you'll need to refer to your estimate of your child's current stage of comfortable speaking (from chapter 1) and your completed speaking situations assessment log (from exercise 3.4). You should also pull out your notebook or journal—you'll need it to jot down the ideas you generate as possible steps on your child's conversational ladder.

Identifying Steps for the Conversational Ladder

Each of the three factors—activities, locations, and people—can be considered part of each step on the conversational ladder. In order to identify combinations of these factors that increase in difficulty, it's best to think of each factor individually first. Essentially, you can construct a separate ladder for each factor and then later combine them. You'll apply the same principle to each ladder you build. Begin with a scenario in which your child currently talks in at least a whisper. Then identify other variations of the same factor that become increasingly challenging for your child. The difference (or distance) between each step on the ladder needs to be small enough to allow for *errorless transitions*. When faced with a new step, your child will probably experience a slight increase in anxiety and perhaps change the quality of his speaking (for example, reduce his rate or volume of speaking). However, if the steps are small enough, he will continue to speak when he reaches the next step on the ladder, making an errorless transition from one step to the next.

Construct a Ladder of Activities

Of the three types of ladders that characterize speaking situations, the activity ladder is the one that children with selective mutism typically move up most quickly. In deciding what types of activities you might include on your child's activity ladder, you should consider some basic concepts, described below.

GENERAL COMFORT LEVEL DURING THE ACTIVITY

Consider how comfortable your child is while engaged in the activity itself. In other words, how relaxed does he seem when he is spending time doing the activity? If you want your child to be successful at facing his fear of speaking, you'll need to start with activities that help him feel comfortable or relaxed. As a general rule, a child is most relaxed when he's involved in a familiar activity at which he is proficient. For example, Denzel, an eight-year-old boy with selective mutism, was quite skilled at computer games and sports activities. Arly, a six-year-old girl, preferred to spend her spare time drawing and coloring. What does your child like to do in his spare time at home? The activities he most often chooses are likely to be rated highest on the fun scale. If your child enjoys an activity and regularly spends time at it, he's likely to feel more relaxed and confident during that activity.

Physical activities. As is the case with most types of fear or anxiety, children with selective mutism often become physically tense when feeling uncomfortable or anxious. If your muscles are tense, it's hard to feel physically (or mentally) relaxed! As a general principle, then, activities that reduce muscle tension may lead to an overall state of relaxation or comfort. If you have a child who enjoys physical activities like sports, you might want to consider adding some athletic activities to your list. Denzel, for example, enjoyed a good game of basketball or baseball. Do remember, however, that if your child isn't drawn to physical activities or perhaps is physically uncoordinated, these activities may actually cause him to become more tense or uptight when asked to participate. That was the case for Arly. Although she had good fine-motor coordination and worked well with her hands, Arly had difficulty with gross motor coordination and had trouble kicking a soccer ball. Because her confidence was low and she felt anxious about her abilities, she preferred to avoid most sports or other activities that required physical coordination.

Academic activities. For most children with selective mutism, many aspects of the school experience become tied to their fear of speaking in that setting. It makes sense then that academic activities such as reading aloud or rehearsing math facts can themselves become triggers for anxiety. Even if your child is a strong reader or a math whiz, these kinds of activities may lead to increased anxiety (or a decreased comfort level) when speaking. Although it'll be important for your child to ultimately feel comfortable talking during such activities at school, you might want to reserve academic activities as higher steps on your child's activity ladder. Of course, you'll also want to think about your child's own natural areas of strength. Is he a competent reader, or does he feel more confident in mathematics and science? And, of course, you'll want to rank each of these activities according to how comfortable (or anxiety-provoking) it will be for your child.

AMOUNT OF SPEAKING INVOLVED IN THE ACTIVITY

Clearly, some activities are more likely to encourage talking than others. For example, when playing video games, Denzel might be focused on the game itself and not welcome conversation. Arly, the young artist, on the other hand, might enjoy a chance to talk to others about her drawing as she works. As you generate your list of possible activities to be included on the activity ladder, think about how much talking the activity encourages.

In general, you should consider activities with low speaking demands (those that require limited speaking) as the first steps on the ladder. Asking your child a closed question (that is, questions requiring single-word responses) is an example of an activity with a low speaking demand. A game of I Spy in which your child has chosen the secret object in the room would be another example of a low-speaking-demand activity.

Medium-speaking-demand activities might include tasks that involve somewhat more verbalization but tend to rely on scripted, predictable language. Counting aloud, reciting the days of the year, naming pictures, completing others' sentences, or even reading simple text aloud might be considered examples of activities with medium speaking demands.

Activities with high speaking demands will be the last steps for your child to practice, after he's become comfortable with less-demanding activities. An example of an activity with high speaking demands might include responding to open-ended questions, where lengthier responses are required. Other examples could include child-initiated conversations, responding to ambiguous or challenging questions, or sharing his opinion on a subject aloud. Keep in mind that high-speaking-demand activities are often characterized by the need for lengthier oral responses and involve more risk taking on your child's part. That is, your child's speaking becomes more open-ended in its content and is subject to opinion—there isn't just one right way for your child to orally respond or participate in the activity. If you're looking for some inspiration about what you might add to your child's activity ladder, you might refer to *The Selective Mutism Resource Manual* (Johnson and Wintgens 2001), which includes a creative list of activities designed to encourage your child to talk while having fun.

Exercise 7.1   Making a List of Activities for Your Child's Activity Ladder

Take out your notebook or journal. Write down a list of activities that might help your child practice speaking at school. Think of activities that might encourage play and conversation. Remember to consider activities that your child often chooses to do in his spare time at home. Think about whether physical activities would be a good choice for him, and make sure to include academic-type activities that could become later steps on the ladder. Have you missed any good ideas for activities? Don't forget that other members of the management team might have some good options to add to your list. See if you can come up with a total of ten to fifteen different activities that your child could participate in within the school setting. Next, review and rate each activity according to the amount of speaking it might encourage, using a chart similar to the one below. Be sure to make room for lots more activities than we've demonstrated in our abbreviated example here.

Description of activity		How much speaking does it encourage?			
		None	Little	Some	Lots
1.	Playing a board game he often plays at home			X	
2.	Playing a game of catch		X		
3.	Reading a short story aloud and answering brief questions				X
4.					

How does your activity list look? Were you and your child's management team able to come up with a range of activities that differ in the amount of speaking they encourage? Keep your list handy because you'll need it for the next exercise in which you'll construct an activity ladder based on your rankings.

Exercise 7.2 Constructing Your Child's Activity Ladder

Once you've assessed all of the activities for the extent that they encourage speaking, you can now arrange the steps in order on your child's activity ladder. Use your notebook or journal to record the order in which the activities should appear on the activity ladder. Make sure that the first steps are activities that your child is already comfortable doing (and ones that require less speaking) and that the last activities are most similar to school-type activities (and ones that require more-extensive speaking demands). As soon as possible, meet with your management team and see if the members agree on the general order of the steps on your child's activity ladder.

Here's a sample of the first and last few activities from Denzel's activity ladder:

Denzel's activity ladder	
1.	Play a game of basketball outside on the playground.
2.	Play a board game that he usually plays at home and requires simple verbal responses.
* *	
8.	Read a story aloud to Denzel and ask him closed questions (e.g., "What's the dog's name?").
9.	Read a story aloud to Denzel and ask him open-ended questions (e.g., "What do you think will happen next in the story?").
10.	Have Denzel read a short story aloud and answer closed questions.

| 11. | Have Denzel read a short story aloud and answer open-ended questions (e.g., "What character did you like best in the story, and why?"). |
| 12. | Have an open-ended conversation with Denzel during an academic activity (e.g., freely chat during work on an art project). |

Construct a Ladder of Locations

With the activity ladder constructed, let's now think about your child's ladder for speaking locations. Back in chapter 1, we introduced the idea that physical location is a factor that often influences how comfortable children are when speaking. The simplest example of this would be to look at your child's comfort level when speaking at your home compared to his comfort level when speaking at the school. It's probably pretty clear that your child is more comfortable, and speaks more freely, at home. Within the school setting too, there are probably differences in your child's confidence when speaking. In deciding on the school locations you might include on your child's location ladder, you should consider that children with selective mutism are most likely to first talk at school in situations that are more private, are visually different from the classroom, and have not been associated with demands to speak.

CONSIDER THE PRIVACY FACTOR

For most children with selective mutism, a specific fear of being heard or seen speaking causes significant distress. So it makes sense to shape the first steps on your child's conversational ladder so that they don't cause your child to be observed or overheard while speaking at school. Can you think of places at school where your child is less likely to be seen, overheard, or interrupted while talking? For example, some children may find a corner of the library to be a more private location than a busy hallway. Within the school building, there are probably rooms that are quieter and see less traffic from students and school personnel. Are you familiar with the layout of your child's school? This is another great example of how school staff (as members of your management team) can be helpful in planning the intervention program for your child. Perhaps school staff members know of a utility room, nurse's room, or other classroom that is not regularly in use.

Even in rooms that are subject to traffic, the level of privacy can be modified. For example, a bookcase or portable partition can visually block the area from the rest of the room. Where your child sits in relation to other structures in the room can also increase or decrease his perceived privacy level. Imagine your child sitting near the door of the library, where he can see out into the hallway (and others can see into the room). Now, imagine your child sitting in a back corner of the library, away from the door, with his back to the rest of the room. In which situation do you think he'd feel most comfortable speaking? We suspect you'd agree with us that the second scenario would be much more inviting for first conversations!

As your child moves up his location ladder, you can then think of the privacy factor in reverse. How can you make a physical location at school a little less private in order to challenge your child more? Could a door that is normally closed be left open a little? Could your child be working at a desk closer to the front of the room where he faces the hallway? You are only limited here by the extent of your creativity and the flexibility of school personnel.

FINDING NONCLASSROOM LOCATIONS AND NOVEL PLACES

It's likely that anxiety has been tied to speaking situations at school for your child since he first enrolled. In other words, every time he has experienced a pressure to speak at school, he has made an association between that situation (activity, location, and persons involved) and an unpleasant feeling of anxiety. It's also likely that the actual classroom setting is the place where your child has experienced the most anxiety about speaking.

In thinking about locations for your child's ladder, begin with places at the school that are different from the classroom, especially those that look different. A great example of a school location that is different from the classroom is the playground. Can you think of rooms in the school that are set up differently from your child's classroom? Maybe the gym, the music room, or an unused meeting room would be good choices as first steps on your child's location ladder. Think too about school locations that are at a physical distance from the actual classroom. The farther away from the classroom the location is, the more likely your child will feel comfortable speaking in that setting.

Relatively novel locations within the school can also be good choices for first steps on your child's location ladder. If he has not spent time in the setting before, it's unlikely that he has associated that locale with the anxiety elicited by a pressure to speak. Can members of your management team help you identify places in the school where your child does not typically spend time during his regular routine?

Exercise 7.3   Making a List of Locations for Your Child's Ladder

Take out your notebook or journal. Write down a list of locations at school where your child could safely spend time when practicing speaking comfortably. Think first of locations that are quieter and are high on the privacy factor. Remember to think about school locations that don't look like a classroom and places that are relatively new to your child. See if you can come up with approximately ten to fifteen different locations at the school. Don't forget that other members of the management team might have some good ideas to add to your list.

How does your list of possible locations look? Were you and your child's management team able to come up with a range of locations at the school that differ in privacy, novelty, and similarity to the regular classroom? Just as you did for the activity ladder, you'll need to have your list of locations handy for the next exercise. Read on!

Exercise 7.4   Constructing Your Child's Location Ladder

Once you've assessed all of the locations for the level of privacy they afford, their similarity to the classroom, and how novel they'd be to your child, you can now arrange the steps in order on your child's location ladder. Use your notebook or journal to arrange the order of locations for this ladder. Make sure that the first steps are locations in which your child will be comfortable speaking now (even if only at a whisper) and end with situations within the actual classroom. As soon as possible, meet with your management team and see if they agree about the places you've chosen and the general order of steps on your child's location ladder.

Below is a sample of the first and last few steps on Arly's locations ladder:

Arly's locations ladder	
1.	The playground
2.	Back corner of the library
3.	Middle of the library
4.	Front of library, next to the door
5.	Utility room at far end of hallway
*	
*	
8.	Back corner of classroom, with a mobile chalkboard screening the class, and Arly facing away from the chalkboard
9.	Back corner of classroom, with a mobile chalkboard screening the class, and Arly facing the chalkboard
10.	Back corner of classroom, with no chalkboard, and Arly facing away from the class
11.	Back corner of classroom, with Arly facing forward in class

Construct a Ladder of People

The final factor you should consider when building the conversational ladder for the school setting is people. This is often the most challenging ladder for children with selective mutism to climb. A change in the person your child is to speak with is likely a greater challenge than a change of activity or location. That's why children with selective mutism often climb the activity and location ladders with one person before starting again with a new person.

As we described to you in chapter 1, we find that the majority of children with selective mutism are likely to first talk to their parent(s) at the school. Next, children with selective mutism typically speak to their peers. Later, after practice speaking with many schoolmates, the child with selective mutism may be ready to speak to adults at school. Even then, the child often works through a ladder of people—perhaps speaking to a parent volunteer, a student teacher, an office staff member, and finally to the classroom teacher when he is comfortable doing so. He starts with adults who are less connected with an anticipated pressure to speak. Of course, if your child seems to be more comfortable with school personnel than with peers, the same principle would apply, but in a different order. Your child could start by speaking to various adults at the school and then later expand his ability to speak comfortably to his classmates, one by one.

In exercise 3.4, you completed a speaking situations assessment log in which you identified the people with whom your child currently speaks, across all different settings. Find your completed log and review it now. If your child hasn't yet started to work through his selective mutism, you may have found that there's a very short list of people in his life whom he speaks to comfortably. Immediate family members and certain children and adults in the community may appear on the list; classmates and school personnel may not. On the other hand, if your child has begun to overcome his selective mutism, some people from the school might already make the list. For example, perhaps your child will on occasion speak in a quiet voice to a classmate on the playground or whisper, "Here," when a substitute teacher takes attendance.

Exercise 7.5   Making a List of Conversational Partners Available at the School

Take out your notebook or journal and find the exercises you completed in chapter 3. Specifically, find the list you made of the people with whom your child currently speaks, and the speaking situations assessment log you completed in exercise 3.4. With this information in front of you, rank people beginning with those your child speaks to most frequently. The people ladder usually begins with parents and immediate family members. Next, list persons your child speaks to on occasion. For example, Denzel speaks to boys in the neighborhood during basketball games, and Arly speaks to a few girls at dance class. Finally, list persons your child currently avoids talking to. The classroom teacher is typically the most anxiety-provoking person on the ladder and is perhaps the last individual your child will come to feel comfortable speaking to at school. Think of each person as a potential *conversational partner*—that is, a person with whom your child could practice speaking with confidence.

With your list made, go back and identify people who could interact with your child at the school. This is an important task, since at this point in the program you want to make your child's ladder specific to the school setting. The fact that your child is comfortable speaking to the grocery store clerk is important to note, but it's unlikely that the clerk will be available to serve as a conversational partner at the school, where your child has the most difficulty. For now, let's focus on the school and the people your child could speak to in that setting.

Here's a look at part of the people list created by Arly's parents:

Person	Could this person be a conversational partner at school?		
	Yes	No	Maybe
1. Mom and Dad	X		
2. Younger sister			X (Could a parent bring her to school?)
3. Grandma			X

4.	Janie (enrolled in same dance class and same class at school; has come over for a playdate)	X		
5.	Nathan (neighborhood friend; attends a different school)		X	
6.	Ms. Simpson (babysitter)		X	

What did you think of the list of people Arly's management team generated? Did it give you any ideas regarding people you might add to your own child's list of potential conversational partners? Keep your list of people out because you'll need it when you build your child's people ladder in the exercise to follow.

Exercise 7.6   Constructing Your Child's People Ladder

Once you've identified people your child could practice speaking with and you've assessed their availability to visit the school on a regular basis, you can now arrange the steps in order on your child's people ladder. Use your notebook or journal to record your list of people. As we noted before, make sure that the first steps are people with whom your child currently speaks comfortably, and then move on to people your child has spoken to on occasion. The last people on the ladder should be individuals with whom your child does not currently speak. In all likelihood, the classroom teacher will be at the top of your child's people ladder. As soon as possible, meet with your management team and see if they agree on the people you've chosen and the general order of the steps on your child's people ladder.

Below is a sample of the first and last steps from Arly's people ladder for school:

Arly's people ladder	
1.	Mom
2.	Dad
3.	Mom or Dad with younger sister
4.	Grandma
5.	Janie
* *	
8.	Christina (classmate)
9.	Hunter (classmate)
10.	School secretary
11.	Teaching assistant
12.	Classroom teacher

COMBINING THE ACTIVITY, LOCATION, AND PEOPLE LADDERS

With the groundwork laid for your child's activity, location, and people ladders, you can now consider combining them into a single, integrated ladder for the school setting. This will become your child's *conversational ladder*. There are many ways in which this can be done. Regardless of how the three ladders are combined, each step on the conversational ladder will represent a speaking scenario at school that involves an activity, location, and person you've identified and represents a situation in which you'd like your child to have practice speaking with confidence. When he's able to speak comfortably in one situation, he can then be encouraged to move up to the next step.

Remember that your child will likely be able to work up the activity ladder more quickly than he does the location or people ladders. The people ladder will probably be the most challenging to climb. So, you may want to make it so that the first several steps on the combined ladder incorporate the same person but change the activity and then the location.

Consider the first draft of the combined ladder a preliminary plan for the first steps on the conversational ladder. Realistically, your child will need to climb up many sequences of steps that expand the situations in which he speaks with confidence. Later steps may need to be modified as your child works up the ladder and you collect more information about your child's fear of speaking and his ability to work through it. For example, you may find that he is comfortable almost immediately with activities that are more academic in nature—as long as they take place in a private location at the school. If he's able to talk at school while involved in academic activities, then he may not need to first practice comfortable speaking while engaged in games he usually plays at home. Although you've carefully estimated where your child might need to start on each of the activities, location, and people ladders, your child himself will ultimately demonstrate his readiness to move to the next step of each.

Exercise 7.7   Developing an Integrated Conversational Ladder for Your Child

Take out your notebook or journal. Keeping in mind what you've learned about how to combine your child's activity, location, and people ladders, see if you can set up the first several steps of your child's integrated ladder. Think about each step as a school scenario in which your child could practice speaking comfortably. Remember that your ideas will represent a preliminary plan that will quite likely need to be modified based on your child's readiness, as well as practical issues that may arise at the school. As soon as possible, meet with your management team and see if they agree about the suitability of the first steps on your child's conversational ladder.

The table below shows the first steps of the integrated conversational ladder that Arly's parents developed. Notice that the first steps focus on changes in activity and location, but that the person involved with Arly remains the same. One step at a time, Arly will practice speaking in scenarios where the activity changes frequently and the location changes somewhat more slowly. Arly will be given lots of practice speaking to her mother during different activities and in different school locations. Once she's successful at that, her management team might give her the chance to practice going up a similar ladder of activities and locations but this time with her dad. When Arly feels comfortable speaking in different situations at school with the family members on her people ladder, she could start again with the first classmate on the list. What do you think of their plan?

Arly's integrated ladder			
Step	Person	Location	Activity
1.	Parent with Arly alone	School playground	Both play I Spy on the playground.
2.	Parent with Arly alone	Back corner of the library	Both play I Spy and board games from home that require simple verbal answers from Arly.
3.	Parent with Arly alone	Middle of the library	Arly draws or colors; parent asks simple questions about drawing.
4.	Parent with Arly alone	Front of library, next to the door	Arly draws or colors to start; parent reads story and asks simple questions.
5.	Parent with Arly alone	Utility room at far end of hallway, away from the classroom	Parent reads story and asks simple questions.
6.	Parent with Arly alone	Utility room at far end of hallway, away from the classroom	Parent reads story and asks first simple questions and then more open-ended questions.

7.	Parent with Arly alone	Utility room at far end of hallway, away from the classroom	Parent reads story and asks open-ended questions; Arly reads story to parent.
8.	Parent with Arly alone	Utility room at far end of hallway, away from the classroom	Arly reads story to parent and discusses story aloud.
9.	Parent with Arly, either during class or before or after school	Back corner of classroom, with Arly facing away from the class	Arly completes drawing task; both play a board game that requires simple verbal answers from Arly.
10.	Parent with Arly	Back corner of classroom, with Arly facing away from the class	Both play a board game that requires simple verbal answers from Arly; parent reads story and asks simple questions.
11.	Parent with Arly	Back corner of classroom, with Arly facing away from the class	Parent reads story and asks open-ended questions; if Arly is ready, she reads a short story to her parent.

A Final Word (or Two) About Your Child's Conversational Ladder

As you can see from looking at Arly's example, the steps of the ladder tend to be small and very gradual. There are many steps on a conversational ladder; in fact, you might think of the conversational ladder as a series of speaking situations (which vary by activity and location) practiced with one person at a time. Fearful speaking situations at school are faced gradually, working from less-anxiety-provoking to more-anxiety-provoking scenarios. As long as your child talks (at least in a whisper) in each scenario he tries, your child is ready to practice that speaking situation until he becomes confident. However, if your child isn't able to speak at all in a new scenario that's introduced, it's important that you insert a smaller step on the ladder in its place immediately. You can expect your child to experience a slight increase in anxiety as he climbs the ladder. After all, he's moving from things that he can successfully do to things that are harder for him. But you want to ensure that the steps on the ladder are small enough that your child's speaking can be successfully transferred to each new situation. You don't want to place your child in a situation that's too challenging for him too early in the process. Not only could that be highly distressing to your child, but he might also need additional time to overcome the additional anxiety he experienced.

As we've mentioned before, your child will overcome his selective mutism through gradual, small steps. Ensuring your child's success, however, will require much patience from everyone involved. Although there's no hard-and-fast rule about this, our clinical experience suggests that children working up a conversational ladder often need more than one school year to overcome this condition. The good news is that, as your child becomes confident in each speaking situation, it's likely that he will not experience unmanageable anxiety tied to that scenario ever again. With each small step your child takes to overcome his mutism, he will also achieve speaking success. In chapter 11, we'll discuss in more detail how certain factors can influence your child's rate of progress.

If you've been able to read this chapter and make sense of the principles of graduated exposure, transfer of confidence from one situation to another, and the conversational ladder, congratulations to you! You're now familiar with the primary components of the intervention program that we'll focus on in the remainder of this book. However, if you find that you're still a little unclear about the construction of the conversational ladder and how it works, don't worry. We've presented a lot of information in this chapter. Given how critical the conversational ladder is to later chapters of the book, we recommend that you take some extra time to reread any sections of this chapter that remain unclear. Once you've done that, you'll probably find yourself wondering how you can put the conversational ladder into practice. In that case, you're ready for the next chapter, which focuses on setting up conversational visits at the school.

8

Setting Up Conversational Visits at School

CHAPTER OBJECTIVES

In this chapter you will learn the following:

★ What a conversational visit is, its purpose, and when it would be helpful to a child with selective mutism

★ How to identify potential partners for conversational visits to the school

★ How to decide what time of day to hold the conversational visits, where to hold them, and what activities might be appropriate choices

★ How to explain conversational visits to school staff and why it's important to coordinate visits in advance with staff

★ How to explain conversational visits to your child

By this point in the book, you probably have a good sense of the basic principles of the program, and you've probably laid the groundwork for a version tailored to your own child's needs. With the help of your management team, you've developed a conversational ladder for your child that considers the people involved, the physical locations for speaking, and the activities during which speaking can occur. Each step on the conversational ladder represents a new situation that integrates one rung of the people, locations, and activity ladders you previously constructed. By combining steps from the single ladders, you can provide your child with many different situations in which she can learn to talk comfortably at school.

Once your child is feeling comfortable about talking in simple situations, she can be encouraged to gradually take additional small steps toward new, more challenging situations. Through gradual steps, your child can transfer her ability to speak comfortably to an expanding range of scenarios. Having conversational visits, a strategy that we'll focus on in this chapter, is an effective way for you to help your child climb the conversational ladder one step at a time.

WHAT ARE CONVERSATIONAL VISITS?

If your child isn't talking on a regular basis at school, then she probably has few opportunities to work through her fear of talking in that setting. As we've discussed previously, it's likely that your child will go through much of her school day avoiding speaking situations that make her anxious. As a result, her fear of speaking may persist or even intensify. To help your child overcome her fear of speaking, it's important that she has opportunities to practice speaking comfortably at school. If those opportunities don't present themselves during the regular routines of the school day, then it will be useful for your management team to consider alternatives. Conversational visits can be used to provide your child with practice opportunities that would not otherwise exist. They offer a way to help your child take the first steps up her conversational ladder at a time when she's uncomfortable speaking to anyone she interacts with during her regular school day.

When Are Conversational Visits Helpful?

Conversational visits are often critical in the early phases of the intervention when your child is just starting to face her fear of speaking at school. If your child isn't speaking to anyone at school, or does so infrequently, conversational visits can kick off the intervention program. Conversational visits can provide your child with a successful experience in which she actually talks with minimal anxiety to someone at school.

Each word your child utters at school represents a step toward overcoming her mutism. Each time your child talks, the skill of speaking comfortably at school is strengthened. As your child speaks more frequently, her fear of speaking will diminish and her confidence will grow. With continued practice, she'll be able to gradually transfer her ability to talk comfortably to situations involving classmates and school staff with whom she currently doesn't talk.

HOW DO YOU IDENTIFY POTENTIAL CONVERSATIONAL PARTNERS?

Conversational visits typically involve the participation of individuals whom your child speaks to comfortably in a setting other than school. These individuals can be viewed as *conversational partners*— people who will provide your child opportunities to practice having relaxed conversations within the school setting. Immediate family members are often good choices as first conversational partners. However, depending on your child, a variety of people might be appropriate choices as conversational partners for school visits. Take out your notebook or journal and review the list of conversational partners you generated in chapter 7. In that exercise, you were asked to identify people your child speaks to with confidence in other settings and then to assess their availability to visit the school. In reviewing the list, you'll probably notice that you, the parent, were identified as a prime candidate, since your child talks to you comfortably and you're most likely to make the time to visit the school. Realistically, you're also the person most devoted to helping your child overcome her fear of speaking.

But, conversational visits can be conducted by others too. For example, you might bring along a younger sibling to a visit, or a grandparent might have time to be involved. It's not necessary for a single person to make conversational visits to the school. In fact, if several people are involved, your child is likely to have more opportunities to practice comfortable speaking. Conversational visits can also be offered by different people on different days. For example, Keith, a six-year-old in first grade, enjoyed visits from his mother and father on different days of the week. In the case of Natasha, a seven-year-old in second grade, her younger brother joined the sessions with her mother, and on occasion her grandmother made visits to the school as well. Because your child may respond differently to the personality and conversational style of each person, different individuals provide a broader range of practice opportunities.

In some instances, a staff person from the school or school board may offer to take on the role of conversational partner. We've heard of special-education teachers, counselors, and speech-language pathologists offering their time in this capacity. If such resources are available to your child at school, that's great! And if such a staff person isn't regularly at the school or if your child hasn't associated this person with a perceived pressure to speak, she may speak comfortably with this individual in no time.

However, more often than not, a staff person may not be available to assume this role. Or, your child may be somewhat reluctant to speak with this unfamiliar person at school. As a result, she may need to spend a significant amount of time with this person before she'll actually feel comfortable speaking aloud. Although all efforts to encourage your child to speak at school will benefit her, we urge you to consider how you or other members of your family can also take an active role in helping your child. Regular conversational visits with a family member, for example, can serve as a complement to the time your child spends with a staff person working through her fear.

AT WHAT TIME SHOULD CONVERSATIONAL VISITS TAKE PLACE?

As a general principle, your child will overcome her fear of speaking more quickly if conversational visits occur frequently and are as long as possible. As is the case when your child learns any new skill, such as playing the piano or learning to swim, practice is essential. The more practice opportunities your child has, the sooner her skills will be strengthened. Beyond that, the time of day for conversational visits really depends on the availability of the visiting conversational partner and your child's classroom routines. For example, an after-school conversational visit might be a good option as a first step on the ladder. After the school day has ended, you'll encounter much less noise and fewer interruptions, and you and your child can move more freely throughout the school.

Because conversational visits will typically need to take place during the school day, make sure to coordinate with school staff members from your child's management team so they can suggest times that would work best. For example, Natasha's classroom teacher suggested that conversational visits take place at the beginning of the day before important class instruction got underway. Keith's classroom teacher invited his father to visit during a less-structured period near the end of the day. Do you know how your child's day is scheduled in the classroom? If your child is in the primary school years, class instruction may be less formal and there may be more flexibility regarding when a conversational visit could take place. If your child is older, it'll be particularly important to find out when critical class lessons are offered so as not to disrupt your child's learning.

Exercise 8.1   Identifying Times for Conversational Visits

Take out your notebook or journal and write down possible times of day that you or another person might visit the school. Use your imagination! Consider times before school, during recess and lunch, after school, and during the evening. Think of the different people who might visit at these times. With your list of possibilities in hand, discuss these with your child's classroom teacher and management team to identify the best options. Keep a record of the times for conversational visits that will work best for all parties. Here's an example of what Natasha's management team came up with:

	Possible time for visit	Day of the week	Person available for visit
1.	In the morning before school (30-minute visits)	Tuesdays and Wednesdays	Mom
2.	In the morning before school (45-minute visits)	Mondays	Mom and Natasha's younger brother
3.	Before afternoon recess (40-minute visits)	Alternating Fridays	Grandma

WHERE SHOULD CONVERSATIONAL VISITS TAKE PLACE?

In chapter 7, we reviewed the importance of location as a factor that can affect your child's comfort level around speaking at school. If you recall, we asked you to generate a list of school locations in which your child could safely spend time to practice speaking comfortably. Take out your notebook or journal and find the location ladder you built (see exercise 7.4). Each location you identified with your management team is likely to be a good choice for conversational visits.

In general, remember that conversational visits should start in a location where your child will talk comfortably right away (even if only in a whisper). Your child will most likely speak first in school settings that are relatively novel and visually different from the classroom, and haven't been previously associated with demands to speak. She'll also be more relaxed if you start your conversational visits in a setting where she won't be seen, overheard, or interrupted by others. When your child is able to speak comfortably to a conversational partner in that setting, you can consider moving up a step on the location ladder to a somewhat more challenging location.

WHAT ACTIVITIES CAN BE USED FOR CONVERSATIONAL VISITS?

When building your child's conversational ladder in chapter 7, you also spent some time thinking about activities that might encourage her to speak comfortably, and you identified specific activities your child might enjoy. Take out your notebook or journal and find the activity ladder you constructed in chapter 7 (see exercise 7.2). Review the activities you thought would be useful for conversational practice with your child at school. During conversational visits with your child, these activities could be used to encourage speaking by helping her be relaxed at school.

It'll also be important for you or others taking on the role of conversational partner to prompt your child to talk as often as possible. It will not be helpful for your child if she sits silently with you during your visit. What can you do to draw her into a conversation? We think you can encourage speaking by showing interest in what she is doing, by naming materials she's playing with, by describing her activities, by making eye contact, or by asking specific questions about the activity you're engaged in. However, what you don't want to do is wind up forcing or coercing your child to speak by insisting that she do so. That would just increase her anxiety and fear about speaking at school, which would be counterproductive. Instead, be relaxed, be yourself, and have fun with your child.

TRACKING YOUR CHILD'S COMFORT LEVEL DURING CONVERSATIONAL VISITS

As you or other conversational partners visit the school, you'll find it informative to track your child's general comfort level both within sessions and from one session to another. We suggest that you make several photocopies of the following log and use it to keep track of how comfortable your child seems during each visit. You can rate her overall comfort level at the end of each visit on a scale of 0 to 10: write "0" if your child seems very uncomfortable and unable to speak, "5" if she seems somewhat comfortable (for example, speaking in a

Tracking progress during conversational visits

Comfort level

10								
8								
6								
4								
2								
0								

Minutes per visit

60								
50								
40								
30								
20								
10								
0								

Date

Key: 0 = quite uncomfortable, unable to speak; 5 = somewhat comfortable; uses a quiet voice; 10 = relaxed, friendly conversation quiet voice), or "10" if she seems relaxed and able to engage in normal conversation. By shading in blocks on the log, you can visually represent your child's comfort level across sessions. Do note that you can also track the length of each conversational visit and the date it occurred.

We encourage you, and others involved in conversational visits, to fill out the form after each visit. You can then share this information with your management team during upcoming meetings.

EXPLAINING CONVERSATIONAL VISITS TO YOUR CHILD

Children with selective mutism typically prefer to be prepared for changes in their routines, including the sudden appearance of a family member at their school. It'll be important that, in collaboration with your management team, you consider a credible explanation for the school visits, which may be determined in part by her age or the routines of the classroom. In general, however, we discourage you from directly informing your child that the purpose of the school visits is to get her to talk. Some children with selective mutism may become more anxious or resistant during conversational visits if they feel they'll be pressured to speak. Instead, you might consider using an explanation that emphasizes educational or extracurricular goals. For example, in Keith's first-grade class, a few parents volunteer to assist the teacher on an occasional basis. Keith's father decided to volunteer to help in the classroom and work individually with his son. Keith hasn't questioned his father's visits to the school, since to him it seems that his dad's simply a parent volunteer in the class. Natasha's mother chose to explain her visits to the school as an opportunity to work on Natasha's reading skills and familiarize her younger brother with the school, since he was to begin attending the next year. Do you have some ideas about how you might explain conversational visits to your own child? There isn't just one way to handle this. You have to trust your good judgment and what you know about your child.

EXPLAINING CONVERSATIONAL VISITS TO SCHOOL STAFF

If you've been successful in organizing a management team, it's likely that a staff person on the team can take on the job of informing school staff of your visits as need be. However, if you've been unable to coordinate a team at the school, you'll need to meet with the principal to share your plans. Bringing a copy of this book to your meeting might help with that task.

Security Policies at Your Child's School

Before you have your first conversational visit, make sure you are aware of any security policies at your child's school. Perhaps you'll need to sign in at the main office each time you visit, carry proper identification, or even have a police background check completed prior to your regular visits to the school. Finding out about these policies ahead of time will help your visits go smoothly.

Coordinating School Visits with the Classroom Teacher

If you haven't been able to include school staff members in your management team, it'll also be important to coordinate conversational visits with the classroom teacher. He or she will likely have preferences regarding the time of day that your child would be absent from regular class instruction, taking into account classroom routines and your child's learning needs. Be sure to seek the teacher's input.

CONCERNS REGARDING YOUR CHILD'S REACTION TO YOUR VISITS

In sharing your plans with the classroom teacher, you might also want to give an overview of the purpose of these visits. Particularly if your child is in the primary grades, the teacher may be reluctant to have you visit during the school day, since he or she may worry that your child will become dependent on your presence at the school or find it upsetting when you leave. It's true that some young children do have difficulties separating from their parents during the school day. Some children may also come to expect their parents to join them during the school day on a daily basis.

If your child is young and has had a history of separation anxiety, it's possible that she will have some difficulty separating from you after a conversational visit. However, in general, we believe that the potential benefits to your child will outweigh the potential draw-backs of visiting the school. If you're able to visit the school regularly, your child will come to learn when and for how long she can enjoy your visits. In fact, in addition to providing opportunities for her to practice speaking comfortably, you'll also be giving your child extra practice separating from you. As for your child becoming more dependent on you due to school visits, it's unlikely that this will per-sist over the long term.

Most important, please remind yourself and school staff that conversational visits are a short-term strategy. The purpose of the conversational visit is to help your child climb up the first few steps of the ladder so she can become more comfortable talking at school. Conversational visits will not impede her general functioning at school. Once your child becomes comfortable speaking with a class-mate or a staff person in the school, the role of conversational visits will be less critical to your child's progress. Your child will have the opportunity to practice speaking comfortably with people who are present during the regular school day, and you may choose to stop visiting the school as a result. Like many children with selective mutism, your child may even come to the point when she herself decides that the conversational visits are no longer necessary. As she becomes more comfortable speaking with you at school, she'll become more relaxed and able to interact with schoolmates and staff. As she becomes more confident in her abilities, she will no longer need that sense of security she's been receiving from your presence at the school. Imagine that!

THE PRACTICAL CHALLENGES OF ARRANGING CONVERSATIONAL VISITS

As you read about your potential role in orchestrating conversational visits, you might be thinking to yourself that this is a big job. Certainly, various practical challenges could stand in the way of you helping your child. The obvious practicalities of life, including work commitments, the availability of child care for your other children, and transportation issues, might make it challenging to arrange school visits. You're not alone if you feel that way. However, we encourage you to consider what you can offer. Every opportunity your child receives to talk with you in a relaxed way within the school setting represents another step toward overcoming her fear of speaking. You can share this role with other family members if you're not as available as you'd like. Or you may find that with some creativity you can make yourself more available than you originally thought.

For example, Natasha's parents both worked full-time and were unavailable during the regular school day. Natasha's mother, however, always drove her daughter to school each morning. With some adjustments to the family's morning routine, Natasha and her mother were able to share a thirty-minute conversational visit before school started. Although Natasha's father was unavailable during the school week, he and Natasha made frequent trips to the school playground for conversational visits (and some fun on the swing set!) each weekend. In Keith's case, his father worked afternoon shifts, so he was able to visit the school for twenty minutes in the middle of the day before he headed to work, and Keith's mother would visit the school at the end of the day with his younger brother.

The bottom line is this: Do what you can. The more speaking practice you arrange for your child, the quicker she'll move up her ladder toward speaking confidently at school. Although conversational visits to the school can be time-consuming, the overall time of your involvement will probably be limited. Think of it as a short-term investment with long-term benefits for your child.

9

Expanding Your
Child's Social Circle

CHAPTER OBJECTIVES

In this chapter you will learn the following:

★ The importance of playdates in helping your child overcome his selective mutism

★ How to identify your child's preferred classmates and best choices for playdates

★ How to organize playdates at home with classmates from the school

★ How to build activity, location, and people ladders for playdates

★ How you can encourage speaking between your child and his playmate

The first classmate your child speaks to at school is often someone your child is willing to talk to in other settings. This classmate may be a neighborhood playmate or a peer who participates in the same extracurricular activity in the community on a regular basis. For example, eight-year-old James, a second-grader, has become good friends with his classmate David, who is in the same Boy Scouts troop. Victoria, a seven-year-old in second grade, enjoys bicycling around the neighborhood and doing crafts with her neighbor and classmate Karen. Does your child interact with a classmate outside of school? If your child speaks comfortably with a classmate in other settings, it's likely that his speaking with that student can be transferred to school—given the right opportunities. Even if your child already speaks to several classmates at school, he will be more likely to expand his speaking to include different classmates if he spends time with them away from the school setting.

Why do you think that is the case? We suspect that it comes back to the importance of physical location as a factor that contributes to your child's comfort level when speaking. As we've discussed, the school setting and associated activities are generally most likely to trigger your child's fear of speaking. As a result, spending time with a classmate away from the school (for example, at your home or in the community) is likely to be more comfortable for your child. When he is more relaxed and at ease, he'll be more likely to speak to a classmate. With lots of practice speaking comfortably to that classmate, your child will eventually feel confident enough to speak to him or her within the school setting. In essence, peer interaction can serve as a bridge that helps your child transfer his ability to speak confidently from other settings to the school environment.

Unlike James and Victoria, however, many children with selective mutism don't have regular opportunities to play with classmates outside of school. For example, a child may attend a school outside his neighborhood, and so the peers he plays with in his neighborhood are not his classmates at school. Or a child may live in the same neighborhood as his classmates but not play with them for one reason or another.

Back in chapter 2, we actually identified inconsistency in peer relationships between home and school as a factor that seems to be associated with selective mutism. Take a minute to think about your own child's peer relationships. Are the peers he plays with outside of school the same children he interacts with in the classroom? Even if you can identify children he sees in more than one setting, does your child have regular opportunities to spend time with these peers outside of school? Arranging regular times for your child to play with classmates away from the school can help accelerate his progress.

Regular playdates with classmates are most effective when done in tandem with a school-based plan, such as optimizing seating arrangements and scheduling conversational visits. However, even if you haven't yet tried any of the other strategies described in this book, you can make a big contribution to your child's progress by arranging playdates. The remainder of this chapter will provide tips you can use when taking on the role of social coordinator for your child.

GATHERING INFORMATION ABOUT YOUR CHILD'S PEERS

In order to determine which children at the school might be good conversational partners for your child, you'll want to have a sense of which students he likes. The goal here is to identify children from your child's class whom he likes but does not yet speak to at school. It just makes sense that your child will feel more comfortable with, and ultimately talk to, a peer he enjoys. Think about it: Have you ever felt forced into a conversation with someone you didn't like, perhaps at work or at a social gathering? In those instances, did you find that you wanted to chat at length, or, more likely, did you try to make a quick exit from the conversation? Your child probably feels the same way when spending time with peers he's less interested in or with whom he feels less comfortable.

You can do a little detective work to gather important information about your child's preferred schoolmates. Given the fact that he is likely to be somewhat reserved and shy at school, the staff members may not be able to determine which peers your child likes based on observations alone. You, on the other hand, have the opportunity to learn which peers make suitable companions by listening to your child describe his school experiences during casual, unobtrusive conversations at home.

Exercise 9.1   Identifying Your Child's Preferred Schoolmates

1. In your notebook or journal, make a list of school peers you know your child likes. Remind yourself of any peers your child has identified as his friends, both in the past and in the present. Add the names of peers your child tends to mention a lot when he's talking about school. If you feel unsure of whose names should be on your list, casually chat with your child about kids from his class. Ask him to tell you about the kids he likes to play with, feels comfortable spending time with, and generally likes.

2. Share your list with the management team and see if the staff members have any other ideas. Check in to see what the staffers think about the children you've identified: Do they think any of them would be incompatible with your child? Next, rank how comfortable your child is with each peer based on level of familiarity and speaking history. You might find it helpful to set up a chart that looks something like the one developed by Victoria's management team:

Student	In the same class?	In extracurriculars together or in neighborhood?	Speaks to peer in community?	Speaks to peer at school?
1. Karen	Yes	Yes— neighborhood playmate	Yes	Yes (on playground)
2. Brenda	Yes	Yes—swimming	Yes	No
3. Jennifer	Yes	No	No	No
4. Kristy	No, but at same school	Yes—dance class	Yes	No

3. Looking at the list of peers identified for Victoria, who do you think would make a good first choice as a playdate for her? Remember, the purpose of these get-togethers is not solely to provide Victoria with some fun, but to also offer an opportunity to practice interacting and speaking with a classmate she doesn't speak comfortably with at school. Remember, too, that Victoria is likely to be at ease more quickly with peers she has regular opportunities to interact with in other settings. Given the fact that Victoria is already speaking to her classmate Karen in the neigh- borhood and on the playground at school, extra playdates with Karen may help them to become conversational partners in the classroom. Brenda might also make a good choice for playdates, since she's also in Victoria's class and they already interact every week at swimming classes. Perhaps with planned one-on-one playdates at home, Victoria will become comfortable speaking with Karen or Brenda both at home and eventually in the school setting.

From the list of peers you've generated for your child, can you identify one peer in particular who would be a good choice for play-dates right now? If there's more than one possibility, we recommend that you start with the peer your child will be most comfortable speaking with.

ORGANIZING PLAYDATES WITH SELECTED CLASSMATES

Once you've identified a classmate for playdates, you can now focus on organizing these social opportunities for your child.

Approaching the Parent(s) or Guardian(s)

If you know the parent(s) or guardian(s) of the classmate you've chosen, you may feel comfortable contacting them directly by telephone or when you cross paths with them at the school or at swimming lessons, for example. But if this seems like a daunting task, that's okay too. Many parents have told us that they find it difficult to approach other parents with playdate invitations, perhaps because they're unfamiliar with the family and don't know how to contact them. And, in this day and age, privacy concerns may mean that it's against school policy for your child's classroom teacher to hand out the home phone number of another child in the class. Or you may feel uncomfortable about initiating conversations with others. Remember that children with selective mutism and their parents sometimes have that tendency in common! If you tend to be a little shy or nervous chatting with someone you don't know well, it might be a bigger job for you to approach another parent on your child's behalf. If that's the case, your child's teachers or school staff might be kind enough to help out. For example, Victoria's mother wrote a little note to Karen's parents suggesting their children make a time to get together outside of school, and Victoria's classroom teacher agreed to send the written invitation home with Karen at the end of the school day. Karen's mother then contacted Victoria's parents directly to set up the playdate. Could something like that work in your case?

Booking Playdates

Once you've identified a good choice for a playmate and successfully contacted the classmate's parents, it's important to keep in mind some general principles for the get-togethers. Although your child will benefit from every single playdate you arrange, you'll want to make them frequent events. You should try to have the identified classmate visit your home as frequently and as regularly as possible. It's really the same principle we described in the section on conversational visits to the school. The more practice opportunities you can provide to your child, the sooner he will become comfortable speaking with his classmate from school.

Depending on the age of your child and whether you know the parents you've approached, you may find that your child's playdate comes with a parent escort. That's okay. In fact, it'll give you an opportunity to properly introduce yourself and become more familiar with the other parent. If things go well, you'll probably have an easier time arranging additional playdates in the future.

BUILDING A LADDER FOR PLAYDATES

In chapter 7, we talked at length about how your child can over-come selective mutism by working slowly up a ladder of speak-ing-related situations at school. The ladder can be built using speaking scenarios made up of three factors (people, locations, and activities). As we've discussed, the first steps on the ladder should be scenarios that your child could likely speak in right now and that would trigger only minimal anxiety. Later steps on the ladder should be scenarios where he doesn't speak now, but will later. (But by the time your child reaches those higher rungs on the ladder, he should not find those speaking situations extremely anxiety-provoking anymore.) The same framework can be used to guide your planning for playdates.

Thinking About the People

In these playdates, unlike in regular playdates, you'll probably need to actively participate in the interactions between your child and his classmate. Your participation will probably be essential in the beginning. Remember, although we hope that both your child and his classmate enjoy their time together, these playdates have a special purpose: to provide your child with much-needed practice interacting (both verbally and nonverbally) in a relaxed way with classmates. If your child isn't comfortable with his new playmate right away, you'll need to be there to help make the interaction more comfortable. You'll also need to be present to offer your child a way to first prac-tice comfortable speaking in front of his new playmate, before he moves on to speaking directly to him. (Later in this chapter, we'll offer you some tips on how you can encourage your child's speaking during playdates.)

Once your child has had lots of practice speaking comfortably to his friend during playdates, you can then think about expanding his social circle and starting the process again—identifying another child from the class whom your child doesn't yet feel comfortable speaking to and arranging playdates with that child.

Thinking About Locations

You've already done this to some extent if you've arranged for playdates to take place at your home. You know that your child is probably most relaxed and himself in his home environment, where he is fairly comfortable talking and doesn't worry that he'll be pressured to talk.

LOCATIONS AT HOME

Now, think about the areas in your home where your child tends to spend most of his time. You might want to consider locations that are very familiar to your child and where he feels most at ease. James tends to spend a lot of time in the family room playing video games or watching television; his father's home office, however, is off-limits to the children. Victoria often spends her leisure time at the kitchen table doing crafts, but she doesn't like hanging out in the basement recreation room. Can you identify your child's favorite spots in your home?

The child's bedroom might be a great place to meet with a playdate if that's where he keeps his toys and activities. For some children, however, the bedroom may seem too personal of a place to bring a playdate right away. If that's the case for your child, playtime in your child's bedroom may need to wait until later, when your child has become more relaxed interacting with his new friend. Don't forget about outdoor spaces either. As we've discussed previously, if your child enjoys physical activity this can help him relax; perhaps the children could play in the backyard where there's room to run and play.

Consider how much traffic from other family members can be expected in different areas of your home. In general, we'd recommend that you first look for places that offer some privacy. Some children with selective mutism suddenly become quiet during a playdate when a family member passes by. We've also heard parents mention that a brother or sister can end up taking over the playdate and doing most of the talking. Although siblings can sometimes serve as icebreakers, their presence may also limit practice opportunities for your child with selective mutism. Use your good judgment here. If you have another child who tends to steal the show, perhaps it would be a good idea to make sure that she's otherwise occupied, perhaps at a playdate of her own at a friend's house.

LOCATIONS IN THE COMMUNITY

Once your child is comfortable speaking with his classmate at your home, consider moving the playdates to other community locations, such as the library, a favorite restaurant, or the mall. When your child is ready, a change in location will help to transfer his speaking ability to an expanding range of settings.

As your child's friendship with his classmate grows, it'll also be natural for playdates to occur at the friend's home. If an invitation has been extended to your child and he's open to this experience, that's a great sign, even if he's a little hesitant. You can think of the friend's home as another location in which your child can practice speaking with comfort. Depending on your child's comfort level, you might want to accompany him during the first few visits at the friend's house. This would allow you to keep an eye on your child's willingness to speak to his friend in this new environment. If your child becomes quiet and reserved in this setting, you can help to facilitate conversation just as you did in your own home.

After your child has had frequent playdates with the same friend in various locations, can you think of a final location to take your child and his playdate? Given the fact that your child probably feels most uncomfortable talking with his classmate at the school, it might be worth it to plan trips to the school grounds when he's ready. Perhaps playdates can take place on the playground or even include a little time inside the school after hours, if you can arrange it. Your child is likely to first speak to his classmate at school when he doesn't have to be concerned about being seen or overheard speaking.

Exercise 9.2 Constructing Your Child's Location Ladder for Playdates

Take out your notebook or journal. Keeping in mind some of the tips you've just read, make a list of locations you could use for upcoming playdates. Remember the location ladder you constructed for conversational visits to the school? Do the same thing here. Make sure that the first steps are locations where your child would be comfortable speaking now (even if only in a whisper) and end with situations on the school grounds, if possible.

Here's the list that James's parents came up with for upcoming playdates:

James's location ladder for playdates	
1.	At home—in the family room
2.	At home—in James's bedroom
3.	At home—in the backyard
4.	At the park
5.	At the mall
6.	At the movie theater
7.	At the school—on the soccer field after hours
8.	At the school—on the soccer field during school hours
9.	At the school—on the swing set and jungle gym
10.	At the school—in the library after hours

Thinking About Activities

In order to set up successful playdates, it's very important to plan activities in advance that encourage your child's speaking. In chapter 7, we reviewed the aspects of activities you should consider when selecting those that encourage speaking. In general, you need to consider how comfortable your child will be when engaged in the activity and how likely it is that the activity will result in your child talking (in other words, the speaking demands of that activity). For example, James's parents suggested that he and his classmate spend at least some of their playdate playing interactive video games together. Victoria's mother arranged for her and her playdate to do a favorite craft activity. In addition to thinking about activities that are familiar and enjoyable to your child, don't forget to consider physical activities if your child is so inclined, since movement activities can lead to a reduction in physical tension and related anxiety. If your child is relaxed when playing sports or the like, he's likely to be more comfortable and hence more likely to speak!

As we mentioned in the paragraph above, remember to consider the speaking demands of the activities you choose for your child's playdates. Just as you did when planning conversational visits at school, you'll want to start with activities with limited speaking demands. For example, try to think of activities that don't require much talking, perhaps only single-word or yes/no responses. Board games or card games like Go Fish! might be good examples. Once your child is able to speak comfortably to his playmate during these highly structured activities, you can then plan for activities that involve more talking.

Exercise 9.3   Making a List of Activities for Playdates

Take out your notebook or journal. Write down a list of activities that your child might be able to do during playdates. Think of activities that might encourage play and conversation. Remember to think about activities that your child often chooses to do in his spare time at home, and consider whether physical activities would be a good choice for him. Once you've generated your list, review and rate each activity according to the amount of speaking it might encourage.

For example, take a look at what Victoria's parents came up with:

Description of activity		How much speaking does it encourage?			
		None	Little	Some	Lots
1.	Board game played often at home			X	
2.	Crafts (painting, beadwork)		X	X	
3.	Baking with Mom			X	
4.	Puppet show				X
5.	Bicycling		X		
6.	Touch tag on school playground			X	
7.	Reading aloud in the school library after hours				X

How many possible activities were you able to come up with? Did you think of anything that your child and his playmate would really enjoy? Were you able to identify a range of activities in which the amount of speaking varies? Keep your list of possible activities for upcoming playdates handy: Just as you did back in chapters 7 and 8, you'll be constructing an activity ladder for use during playdates.

Exercise 9.4   Constructing Your Child's Activity Ladder for Playdates

You can now arrange the order of steps on your child's activity ladder for playdates. Use your notebook or journal to record the order of activities for the ladder. Remember that the first steps should be activities that your child is already comfortable doing (and that require less speaking). As we mentioned above, once your child is more comfortable interacting with his new friend during playdates, you can plan for activities that demand more speaking.

Here's a sample from Victoria's activity ladder:

Victoria's activity ladder for playdates	
1.	Doing a craft together (painting? play dough? beadwork?)
2.	Game day (favorite board games and card games)
3.	Baking (with Mom)
4.	Bicycling adventure
5.	Puppet show
6.	Pretend dance recital in the backyard
7.	Swimming at a local recreation center
8.	Fun on the school playground (touch tag, hide-and-seek)
9.	Reading in the school library after hours
10.	Playing "school" in the classroom after hours (remember, you'll need to get permission from a teacher or the principal beforehand.)

COMBINING THE ACTIVITY, LOCATION, AND PEOPLE LADDERS FOR PLAYDATES

Now that you've decided on the people, locations, and activities for your child's playdates, it's time to plan the first few steps on your child's playdate ladder. Just like you did in chapter 7 with conversational visits, you'll now think about ways that you can vary the activity and location during playdates with the same classmate. Each scenario represents a situation in which you'd like your child to practice speaking. Start with scenarios that involve minimal anxiety and that he'll speak in now, and then move to more anxiety-provoking speaking situations where he's currently less likely to speak. When he's able to speak comfortably to his classmate in one planned scenario, you can think about how to stretch his speaking to a new situation during the next playdate.

It's hard to anticipate how comfortable your child will be with his classmate during the first visits to your home. Given the fact that you can't know for sure how quickly your child will be ready to move up all of the steps on the ladder (or the exact order in which he will do so), you should concentrate on the first few steps for now. Once you've had a chance to observe your child during several playdates, you can make decisions about later steps on the ladder. Be prepared to be flexible and creative.

Exercise 9.5   Developing an Integrated Ladder for Playdates

Take out your notebook or journal and think about steps your child could take to practice speaking with a classmate during playdates. Start by focusing on one friend and combine the activity and location ladders to create speaking situations your child could tackle with that friend. Write down your tentative plan about where to start the playdates and what your child might work toward. Remember, your ideas will represent a preliminary plan that may need to be modified after you have a better sense of your child's comfort levels.

Below is a table showing the steps on Victoria's ladder for playdates, combining the activity, location, and people ladders. Notice that the first steps focus on changes in activity within the home. Notice too that Victoria's mother does not need to actively participate in the playdates later on, when her daughter is speaking comfortably to her peer. Would any of these steps work for your own child?

Step	Person	Location	Activity
Victoria's combined ladder for playdates			
1.	Victoria with classmate (with Mom present)	Kitchen	Crafts
2.	Victoria with classmate (with Mom present)	Kitchen	Board games and card games
3.	Victoria with classmate (with Mom present)	Kitchen	Bake cookies!
4.	Victoria with classmate (with Mom present)	Outside of house	Bicycling
5.	Victoria with classmate (with family members invited to watch final performance of puppet show)	Victoria's bedroom	Puppet show (making puppets, writing a story line, and presenting puppet show to audience)
6.	Victoria with classmate (with Mom present)	Classmate's house	Victoria brings a favorite game to play
7.	Victoria with classmate (with Mom as chaperone)	Pick up classmate at her house and then head to the public swimming pool	Victoria and classmate swim during public hours
8.	Victoria with classmate	Trip to the public library	Victoria and classmate read to each other
9.	Victoria with classmate	School playground	Touch tag and time on the swing set
10.	Victoria with classmate	Classroom in school	Play "school" in classroom on a Saturday while custodial staff is in building

YOUR ROLE AS CONVERSATIONAL FACILITATOR

Speaking with classmates at home often occurs through a gradual series of stages or steps. At first, your child may play with his peer but not directly speak to him. Next, your child may allow his new playmate to overhear him speaking to you or other family members. After that, your child may speak to his new playmate by answering or asking questions through you; essentially, you become the go-between or bridge for your child's speaking. Finally, as he becomes more comfortable with his playmate, he may start speaking directly to his peer. Each well-planned playdate will lead to additional comfortable interactions between the children.

When Is Parent Involvement Helpful?

You can play a key role in encouraging practice and building your child's confidence when speaking during playdates. As we mentioned earlier in this chapter, the primary purpose of the playdate is to provide your child with opportunities to become comfortable interacting with a classmate. You don't want your child to become silent and tense throughout a playdate—that wouldn't be any fun for either your child or his new playmate! If your child remains completely mute and inhibited during a playdate, then this is a sign that his anxiety about speaking has essentially been transferred to the home setting. In addition to feeling anxious about speaking to his classmate at school, he now feels uncomfortable speaking in his own home. That's a problem.

This is the reason why you, as a parent, must be actively involved in the first few playdates. You really need to prevent the pattern of speaking anxiety and related avoidance from taking hold at home. How do you know when you need to be actively involved in encouraging speaking during playdates? You should follow the same general principles used for deciding when conversational visits to the school are helpful: If your child isn't speaking at all or does so infrequently during a playdate, then your active participation is important. Just your presence can increase your child's general comfort level, reduce anxiety, and increase the likelihood of interaction between the children. Ultimately, this will help your child move more quickly toward speaking comfortably with his new playmate and ensure a positive experience for both children.

Tips for Encouraging Speaking During Playdates

To encourage your child to practice speaking and help him build confidence, you should look for every opportunity to prompt him to speak in the presence of the new playmate. Although he may not be ready to talk directly to his friend yet, your child could start by speaking to you during the playdates. Through this simple, everyday type of interaction, he can practice getting comfortable with having his playmate see and hear him speak. That's often a good place to start building his confidence so he can later speak directly to his playmate.

Note, however, that children often become more reserved and limit speaking even to their mom or dad when a new playmate is visiting. Perhaps you've noticed that your own child attempts to communicate with you through nonverbal means (for example, nodding or shaking his head or pointing), rather than speaking, or even avoids communicating with you entirely, when there is company in the family home. Without a doubt, if your child is feeling anxious during the playdate, you'll have to put some effort into drawing him out to speak with you.

Although it's important to get your child talking to you during initial playdates, it's also important that you don't give him an ultimatum to speak. We know it's tempting to try to reason a child into talking. Parents may sometimes say things that can be experienced as an added pressure to speak, such as "If you don't talk to your classmate, he will think you don't like him," or "If you don't talk to your new friend when he visits, he won't want to come back to see you again." As well intentioned as they may be, these comments might cause your child to sense an increased pressure to speak, and as a result his speaking anxiety might rise, making him more inhibited when his peer visits. As we've discussed before, the first step in encouraging your child's speaking is to take the pressure off about doing just that! Removing the pressure is likely to lead to an increase in your child's general comfort level when interacting with his play-mate. It also builds his confidence to take the next step: talking to you in his friend's presence.

MAKING COMMENTS AND ASKING QUESTIONS

So how do you encourage your child to speak without directly pressuring him? In chapter 7, we described some techniques you can use to encourage speaking during conversational visits at the school. The same strategies can be used in your role as conversational partner during playdates at home.

Making comments. To first break the ice and facilitate conversation throughout playdates, you might want to simply show interest by com-menting on what your child is doing during play. Below are some examples of comments you can make during playdates. Notice that the comments don't require your child's response but instead fill silences and stimulate interaction (even if nonverbal) between the children

Parent: That's a very colorful painting, Victoria. I like the way you've made the clouds look so fluffy.

Parent: Wow, James, look how well you did at the game! That's your highest score yet! Nicely done!

Balanced attending. Don't forget that, before your child is comfort-able, it's also your job to facilitate conversation with the new playmate so that he or she also feels comfortable. As a way of accomplishing this, you might want to draw attention to the playmate's activity, too, striking up some conversation with the playmate in your child's pres-ence. By doing so, you'll help the playmate enjoy the visit and model conversation skills for your own child at the same time.

Parent: Look, Victoria, do you see how nice Karen's painting has turned out? I love the colors you've used. Is that a picture of your family's dog?

Parent: So David, it looks like you're very good at video games too. Do you play them at home like James does? What are your favorite games? I wonder what's going to happen at the next level of the game?

Parent: You have both painted very interesting pictures.

Asking questions. Once you've had a chance to make comments about the play activity, consider how you can next encourage your child to practice speaking. If he seems quite anxious, you'll probably want to start by giving him opportunities to speak with you in front of his play-date. We suggest that you use questions that require little speaking to begin with. For instance, make use of simple closed questions that require only one-word answers from your child. These are often questions that start with "where," "who," or "what." To reduce speaking demands for your child, you can end each question with two options. That way, your child can answer with only one word, and it's clear to him what might be an appropriate choice. Below are some examples of this type of question that could work well during early playdates:

Parent: Who is this in your painting—your father, or Grandpa?

Parent: Where do you want to work on the craft—at the kitchen table or in the living room?

Parent: Who should roll the dice first—you or your friend?

Parent: What kind of cookies would you like to bake with your friend—chocolate chip or oatmeal?

Parent: What would you like for a snack—a muffin or yogurt?

When the child responds to your question, it's always good to then try to stretch the conversation with him if you can. Let's revisit the snack question presented above, but this time the parent can follow up with further closed questions:

Parent: What would you like for a snack—a muffin or yogurt?

Child: A muffin.

Parent: What kind would you like? We have blueberry and carrot.

Child: Blueberry.

Parent: Where would you like to eat your snack with your friend—in the kitchen or in the family room?

Child: Family room.

Notice that this parent used questions starting with "what" and "where." With practice responding to your simple one-word questions, your child will become comfortable with this type of talking in the presence of a playmate. Once your child consistently responds to your simple one-word questions, you can then move to more open-ended questioning, like the following:

Parent: I'm going grocery shopping tomorrow. I want to pick up some more muffins. What's your favorite type of muffin, if you could choose?

In this case, the parent still asked a question that requires a simple, one-word answer, but the possible response options were not included in the question. Believe it or not, even that subtle difference in questioning can be more challenging for the child with selective mutism. How do you think your child would respond to this type of questioning when a new playmate was visiting your home?

Questions with indirect rewards. Although offering direct rewards for speaking can be experienced as added pressure, we've found that children with selective mutism often first speak when there's an indirect incentive that motivates them to speak. An indirect reward would be any sort of incentive that is unstated but is an outcome of speaking. For example, when a question you pose to your child has a built-in (though unstated) reward for speaking, your child may be more likely to respond. Take a look at the examples above. Can you see how many of these questions might offer an indirect incentive to the child? In general, children often find the opportunity to make a choice about a snack, meal, or activity to be an indirect reward for stating their preference.

CHANGING LOCATION AS NECESSARY

Since the goal of your participation is to encourage your child to speak, you may need to be creative to make that happen. If your child remains silent when you've asked a question that requires little speaking in front of his friend, then you'll need to think of other ways you can reduce his anxiety. Think back to the three factors associated with speaking anxiety—the activity, the location, and the people involved. Are there ways you can lessen the challenge of speaking for your child by adjusting any of the factors?

A change of physical location is often an effective way to further reduce anxiety for your child. Depending on your child's general level of comfort with being heard by his friend, you may have several options. You might be able to simply ask your child to lean over and whisper his response in your ear. If that remains too challenging for your child, you could move yourself over to the corner of the room and ask your child to join you. In both instances, the playmate might not be able to hear your child speak but would certainly see him speaking. That's a step your child may need to take before feeling comfortable having others actually hear his words. If he can become comfortable having his playmate observe him speaking, he may soon be ready to speak in his peer's presence.

If your child is having significant difficulty speaking to you in the scenarios described above, then you may need to actually invite your child into another room. That's okay. You'll want to start with minor modifications to physical location, but if your child is unable to speak, do what needs to be done to get him talking. He needs to first feel comfortable enough to speak to you in any context while a play-mate is visiting the home. Remember that selective mutism is often about a fear of being heard or seen speaking in certain situations. Once your child is able to speak to you in more private situations dur-ing the playdate, you can then adjust physical location gradually. You can set up speaking practice for your child that slowly moves him back to the playmate's presence, so that eventually his playmate can hear his responses to you.

One final note about your role as conversational facilitator: We want to remind you that your approach should be geared to the developmental level of your child. Obviously, your comments and questions will be much simpler in their content when you're interact-ing with younger children. It becomes more challenging for a parent to participate in playdates when the children involved are older and more mature. In the case of an older child, you may still be able to facilitate conversation, but you'll need to gear your participation and your comments in a developmentally appropriate way. For example, rather than sit in on a craft activity with two preteens, you may choose to encourage speaking during a casual snack in the kitchen, or in the car as you taxi the children somewhere. As is the case with many of the strategies described in this book, it's important to respect your child's level of cognitive, emotional, and social development. We'll talk more about the special challenges of supporting older children with selective mutism in an upcoming chapter.

MAKING PROGRESS ONE STEP AT A TIME

In reading the above tips for encouraging speaking during playdates, you were probably reminded that working toward speaking comfortably will happen gradually for your child. In the same way that your child can work step-by-step up his activity, location, and people ladders at school, he can also be helped to work up a ladder that helps him speak with classmates away from school. With your support, he can work from less-anxiety-provoking to more-anxiety-provoking speaking situations involving his new playmate. If your child is unable to speak in a new scenario you've introduced, then he'll need you to create a smaller step on the ladder as soon as possible. You want to build your child's confidence in speaking, so he needs to be successful at every step along the way.

Since each child with selective mutism is unique, we can't predict how quickly your own child will become comfortable during playdates. If your child is already comfortably interacting with his playmate during extracurricular activities in the community, you may find that he starts speaking to that child at home fairly quickly. If he has begun speaking to his classmate in select settings at school (like on the playground), you might also find that he speaks easily to this classmate at your home. In general, if your child tends to be comfortable interacting with same-aged peers, he's likely to work up the playdate ladder fairly quickly. On the other hand, if he tends to feel nervous or uncomfortable in most social situations, then he may take longer to climb that ladder.

The first few playdates will give you important information. You'll get a sense of your child's current comfort level with his peer and the number of steps he'll need to climb on his ladder for playdates. At that point, you can make decisions about how actively involved you need to be to facilitate conversation and offer initial speaking practice for your child, and you can plan the next steps he can take. Once he has become comfortable speaking with his new playmate in a variety of situations, you can then begin planning play-dates with another classmate. Again, it's hard to predict how quickly your child will work through his playdate ladder with a second peer. We suspect that it will have a lot to do with your child's general familiarity and comfort level interacting with each child. That being said, it's likely that your child will generally be more confident once he has already established a friendship and ability to speak comfort-ably with at least one classmate.

Playdates can be a useful strategy to help your child overcome his selective mutism. Your child is more likely to expand his speaking to classmates he spends time with away from the school setting. These social get-togethers, as described in this chapter, are intended to do more than just offer your child some fun. Well-planned playdates with a classmate from school can provide your child with important oppor-tunities to practice speaking and function similarly as conversational visits to the school. Once your child is comfortable speaking to a class-mate first away from and later at school, his momentum for overcoming selective mutism tends to increase. In the next chapter, we'll discuss the importance of momentum as a means to maintain your child's progress and ensure the success of the intervention.

10

Maintaining Your Child's Progress and Ensuring Success at School

---

CHAPTER OBJECTIVES

In this chapter you will learn about the following:

- ★ The importance of monitoring your child's progress over time

- ★ How to develop and use a speaking-situations log to track your child's progress

- ★ How to maintain your child's momentum in working through selective mutism

- ★ The potential role of an incentive system to ensure your child's continued progress

- ★ How to ensure your child's academic success by considering accommodations to your child's program where speaking is required

- ★ Alternative methods that teachers can use to evaluate your child's language-based abilities

★ Your child's educational rights and the process of formally identifying your child as a student with special educational needs

If you've made it to this part of the book and you've used the strategies we've described, we hope that your child has benefited from your efforts. By helping your child climb conversational ladders both in and outside of school, you have given her the opportunity to face her fear of speaking through practice and the patience of those supporting her. Although learning to speak confidently in a wider range of situations may be a gradual process, you may have already begun to see changes. Maybe you've noticed that your child is simply more relaxed about attending school or seems to be enjoying the school experience more than she did. Maybe you've seen more confidence in your child in other settings too.

The parents of Elizabeth, a five-year-old kindergartner, have noticed that she seems generally more comfortable interacting with others. She smiles at the grocery store clerk, she will wave at the mail carrier, and she talks about school with more enthusiasm. Elizabeth's mother and teacher, using the logs from chapter 6 of this book, have also noted significant improvements in Elizabeth's general comfort level during daily activities. At school, Elizabeth separates from her mother more easily in the morning and seems more relaxed to explore classroom activities. Elizabeth spends most of her school time with her classmate Shari, who comes over often for playdates. She's even been spotted giggling and whispering with Shari in the dress-up corner of the classroom.

Anthony, a seven-year-old in second grade, has also shown positive changes. Anthony now chats with his classmate Max, both at soccer practice and in quiet spots at the school. He looks forward to regular playdates with his new friend and has even accepted several invitations to Max's house to play. His classroom teacher has reported that Anthony seems much more comfortable during class time and has become a more active participant in daily lessons. He'll raise his hand to volunteer to write the date on the blackboard in the morning, he's willing to take messages to the office, and he communicates his needs to the teacher through Max, usually whispering or quietly telling Max what he wants the teacher to know. Anthony's classroom teacher was thrilled to hear him quietly murmur "Good morning" to her when entering the classroom the other day.

MONITORING PROGRESS OVER TIME

Although it's important to celebrate each small step your child takes toward overcoming her selective mutism, it's also critical that progress be maintained. As your child climbs her conversational ladder at school (and elsewhere, if helpful), you'll need to carefully monitor her progress and be on the lookout for challenges ahead.

Using Logs to Track Progress

In addition to using the general comfort level logs in chapter 6 (exercises 6.5 and 6.6), you might also want to keep track of the expanding range of situations in which your child will speak, both in and outside of the school setting. If you and your management team have an up-to-date record of what your child can now do, it makes it easier to set new goals for transferring her comfort with speaking to new situations. We recommend that you update your records of your child's speaking successes on a regular basis. Some management teams make it a standard practice to update their records during their monthly team meetings. In other cases, a parent might take responsibility for keeping an updated record, using information collected from school staff members and her own observations. Some parents have found it helpful to actually create a speaking achievements progress log that can be used to systematically keep track of when their child begins to speak to new people, during new activities, and in new locations.

Exercise 10.1   Developing a Record of Speaking Situations

Think about the steps your child has already taken to overcome her fear of speaking. Could you generate a list of all of activities and locations in which your child now talks with relative ease and the people to whom she now speaks? Could you identify all of the speaking situations your child has mastered, both inside and outside of school?

Perhaps you'd find it helpful to develop a speaking achievements progress log for your child. It might be something like the speech situations assessment log you completed in chapter 3 (exercise 3.4), except it would allow you to track speaking patterns with a larger range of people. Here's the log that Anthony's parents developed to keep track of his progress:

Speaking achievements progress log					
Situation	People				
	Mom	Dad	Sister	Max	Classroom teacher
At home					
At the grocery store					
In a restaurant or store					
At soccer practice					
At Max's house					
At school: on the playground					
At school: in the library					
At school: in the hallway					
At school: in the classroom					

When making and using a progress log for your own child, you might find the following suggestions helpful:

- When recording speaking situations, try to be as specific as you can, perhaps breaking each situation down by location and by activity. In the above example, Anthony's management team might have found it useful to specify whether Anthony talks to others in particular locations of the library, such as the back corner, the computer lab section, or near the door, and what types of activities he's doing when he talks.

- In addition to recording the name of each conversational partner, you might also consider keeping track of the date that talking was first observed in each situation.

- Consider building a longer-range progress log that lists not only the people your child currently speaks to but also those who might be the focus of new speaking goals. Some management teams actually write down the first names of all class members and important school staff members on a log of this kind. Having a list of all possible conversational partners can help when your management team is considering next steps on your child's conversational ladder.

When you have some time to devote to the task, take out your notebook or sit down at your computer and see if you can draft a speaking achievements progress log for tracking your child's progress. Once you design your log, you can share it with the classroom teacher and the rest of your child's management team. Do other members of the management team have information you could record? We'd encourage you to check in regularly with school staff to update your child's speaking achievements progress log as your child progresses. Progress is often slow and may extend over much of the current school year and possibly beyond. A detailed log of this kind will provide a way for the management team to track your child's progress over time.

MAINTAINING MOMENTUM

Maintaining momentum as your child progresses is key to ensuring she'll successfully overcome her selective mutism. As we've mentioned previously in this book, there will probably be times of great progress and times of slower momentum and gains—and that's natural. What you want to prevent is a complete standstill in your child's progress.

Remember that your child's selective mutism is like other specific fears or phobias. If the fear is not worked through little by little, it's likely to persist. Often, without even making a conscious choice to do so, your child will tend to speak in situations where she feels comfortable and avoid those situations where she does not. So it's important to keep the momentum as your child reaches for more challenging steps on her conversational ladder. If her work is allowed to slow to a halt after she's made important progress, it will become much more difficult for her to take new steps forward.

Regular Management Team Meetings

There are many ways to ensure continued progress and momentum for your child. Regular management team meetings are very helpful in this regard, since they give you and school staff members ongoing opportunities to discuss your child's progress and identify the next speaking goals. Even if the entire team is unable to meet regularly, it'll still be beneficial for you to check in regularly with primary members of the team, like the classroom teacher.

If those supporting your child have agreed in advance on the next step on your child's conversational ladder, then practice opportunities for that step can be arranged when your child is ready. Sometimes there are practical issues related to an upcoming step that need to be sorted out well in advance, such as arranging upcoming locations in the school for conversational visits, planning changes to seating locations, or pairing another classmate with your child.

Anticipate Obstacles or Changes to the Plan

Another way to ensure continued momentum for your child is to be aware of, anticipate, and plan for any upcoming obstacles to your child's progress.

ABSENCES OF CONVERSATIONAL PARTNERS

At some point, you might be informed that the classroom teacher will be going on leave for a period of time and that a substitute teacher will be filling in. Or maybe you'll realize that you won't be able to participate in conversational visits during the next month because of a busy work schedule. Or perhaps your child's preferred classmate (and playmate outside of school) is moving away from the area permanently. Can the management team decide on different steps on the conversational ladder that can be tackled when key situations, activities, or people are not available?

SCHOOL VACATIONS

Particularly important changes that can be anticipated are breaks in the school schedule. Your child probably looks forward to winter, spring, and summer breaks, but while school is out, the opportunities to practice talking in school-related situations become more difficult to arrange. As a result, it's important to plan ahead for these scheduled breaks in the school year. We'll give you some ideas for how to maintain momentum during school breaks in the next chapter.

The Use of an Incentive System

Throughout this book, we've emphasized the importance of not placing undue pressure on your child to speak before she's ready. You've learned that incentive systems or rewards for speaking can inadvertently add pressure and increase your child's anxiety about speaking. In essence, if an incentive system or offer of reward is poorly planned or timed, it can often backfire by actually discouraging your child from talking! However, you've also learned a great deal about selective mutism and the basic principles behind the strategies we've offered. With that information in mind, let's look at the potential benefits of an incentive system.

WHAT IS AN INCENTIVE SYSTEM FOR?

The reasoning behind an incentive system is pretty straightforward: People are more likely to do something if the act of doing it results in a positive consequence. For example, you've probably discovered that your child is far more likely to do her after-dinner chores if she then gets to watch her favorite television program. Even adults tend to be motivated to head to work daily in anticipation of the paycheck that will follow.

Children are often familiar with incentive or reward systems through their schoolwork (like grades on report cards) and other extracurricular activities (such as those badges Girl Scouts earn). Some parents, however, are hesitant to use incentives, viewing them as bribes for doing things that children should be expected to do independently. If you feel that way, you're not alone. However, an incentive is different from a bribe. Typically, a bribe is a thing you'd give someone to make them do something solely for *your* benefit. In comparison, a reward or incentive is a way to motivate your child to do something that will ultimately be helpful to *her*. Do you see the difference?

Incentive or reward systems can offer your child encouragement to do things that are challenging or unpleasant. For your child with selective mutism, a well-designed incentive system can motivate her to move from one step on the conversational ladder to the next. Incentives can motivate, sustain effort, and offset the stress children may experience while overcoming their fear of speaking.

WHEN IS AN INCENTIVE SYSTEM HELPFUL?

As you know, your child's progress in overcoming her selective mutism can be quite slow and gradual. If your child's progress has reached a plateau, or significant momentum has been lost, an incentive system might be a useful supplemental strategy to ensure continued progress.

It's extremely important to note, however, that an incentive system should only be used after your child has already begun to speak in certain situations where she was previously silent. For example, after some practice, Elizabeth began speaking to her parents during conversational visits to the school. Anthony started speaking to his friend Max in select situations both inside and outside the school. In both cases, a baseline of speaking emerged in situations where it didn't exist before. This is a necessary prerequisite if an incentive system is being considered.

WHAT SHOULD THE INCENTIVE SYSTEM TARGET?

In general, an incentive system can be helpful to the child with selective mutism if it targets her general motivation to face her fear of speaking or social interaction. Incentive plans can be used to increase the frequency of speaking in certain situations and also increase the likelihood that speaking will occur in new settings or with new people.

If you think back to some of the examples of incentives we described earlier in this book, you may now have a better sense of why they tended to go wrong. It's definitely not helpful to offer a reward to a child for speaking in a certain situation if she's never accomplished that before. To comply with such a request is just too big of a step for the child. As a result, the offer of a reward actually could add pressure on the child to speak, increase anxiety, and compound the problem!

In our experience, we've found that a less-direct approach works best. Instead of targeting speaking outright, the most effective incentive systems target a related behavior. For example, Anthony earned points for each book he read aloud to his parent during conversational visits to the school. The target behavior for the reward was reading, rather than speaking per se. However, through this reading program, Anthony was also practicing speaking aloud at school. An older child with selective mutism might earn points for giving correct responses to questions about a book she has read. Again, in this case, the target behavior is reading comprehension rather than speaking aloud in the classroom, but the child ends up practicing speaking in the process. In essence, an indirect incentive system rewards speaking in the context of another activity. As you might imagine, incentive systems of this kind are likely to motivate your child but minimize anxiety because they de-emphasize speaking as the goal.

HOW DO YOU SET UP AN INCENTIVE SYSTEM OF THIS KIND?

There are many good parenting resources available that can walk you through the basic steps of setting up an incentive system. Here are some of the fundamentals you'll need to keep in mind:

- You and your management team first need to decide which behavior(s) you would like to encourage. It's important to select very specific behaviors so it's clear when your child has earned a reward for her efforts.

■ Whenever possible, target behaviors that indirectly result in speaking, such as reading, answering questions about a story, or describing one's artwork.

■ Try to keep the incentive system simple. Too many target behaviors can make it too complicated—one to three target behaviors seems to work best.

■ When you more directly target speaking, be sure to begin with goals that your child can currently accomplish. For example, target more-frequent speaking in situations where your child has recently started to talk, or target speaking in situations that are new but similar to her current successes.

■ Try to reward your child as soon as possible after the target behavior has taken place. It'll be important to have the classroom teacher on board to help out with this, just in case your child earns a reward while at school.

■ When you give your child a reward, it's important that the reasons are very clear. Explain to your child exactly what she did that you liked and why you are proud of her for doing it. For example, say "I liked the way you were able to join the other kids at the swimming pool this week, instead of staying beside me during the class." This is more effective than simply "You did a good job today."

■ In most cases, small, simple, and frequent rewards tend to work better than bigger, less frequent ones.

■ In deciding on appropriate rewards for your child's efforts, identify things that are highly valued by your child. Sit down with your child to discuss possible ideas for rewards. Be sure to decide on reasonable rewards, not things that will break the bank!

■ Incentive plans can include both material rewards (for example, a trip to a favorite restaurant or getting to choose which movie you'll rent) and nonmaterial rewards (for example, praise, one-on-one time with a parent, or going for a long bike ride).

■   When generating reward options, it's also helpful to come up with a few different rewards to prevent your child from becoming bored. Allow your child to select the reward earned from a menu of options.

■   Finally, keep in mind that the best incentive systems balance immediate, short-term rewards with a longer-term source of motivation. For example, in addition to giving the immediate reward of stickers for her efforts, Elizabeth's parents also counted each sticker as a point toward their daughter's longer-term goal: a new pet gerbil!

Many parents of young children create a visual or tangible incentive system, placing a star or sticker on the chart every time the child engages in the target behavior. If you use a reward chart, put it where your child can easily see it and note the progress she's making. For example, Elizabeth's parents offered their daughter a sticker every time she bravely went to swimming lessons, participated in a playdate at her home, or got on the school bus by herself. The reward chart was posted on the refrigerator door, and Elizabeth took great pride in being able to put each sticker on the chart herself. Anthony's classroom teacher kept a chart taped on the corner of his desk. Every time Anthony volunteered to go to the blackboard or answered a question in class (through his friend Max), his teacher put a happy face on his chart.

If you're a parent, we're sure you've had some experience with incentive or reward systems. Parents often report that they've tried this kind of thing before, but with limited success. Although the basic principles of an incentive system are easy to understand, developing a well-planned system for your child is a more challenging job. Members of your management team with expertise in behavior management are often great resources for advice in this regard.

In sum, depending on your child's stage and rate of progress, incentive systems can be a helpful tool to ensure momentum. Although the basic principles for designing any effective incentive system will apply, it's important that you carefully consider how a system that encourages speaking will need to be different for the child with selective mutism. Most children working with an incentive system may not be experiencing anxiety related to target behaviors, but your child probably is. As a result, the incentive system needs to motivate the child to be brave rather than serve as another fear trigger.

In collaboration with your management team, you'll be able to decide whether an incentive system would be helpful to your child. If she is progressing nicely without such a plan, you may choose to continue without. Alternatively, you might choose to establish an incentive system just when things are going well. It's easier to accelerate improvement and prevent plateaus when your child is already making progress. And if your child's progress has slowed significantly or if your child is older (and more avoidant), you may also find that an incentive system helps her face her fear of speaking.

ENSURING YOUR CHILD'S ACADEMIC SUCCESS AT SCHOOL

Despite all of your support and that of the management team, your child will likely need some time to work through her selective mutism. Although it's difficult to forecast how long it'll take for your child to overcome her fear of speaking, it's important to look ahead to future academic expectations and her ability to meet them. In particular, as your child progresses academically, it's likely that the demand for oral communication skills will increase. The management team will need to plan for, and problem solve in advance, difficulties around upcoming academic requirements that involve speaking in challenging situations.

Accommodating Your Child's Academic Programming Needs

Back in chapter 1, we discussed the typical academic progress of children with selective mutism. Despite the understandable worries of parents and school staff, research has not yet shown that selective mutism interferes with academic progress. Children with selective mutism often progress academically at a rate that is consistent with their abilities. As a result, modifications to class lessons are not typically necessary for the child with selective mutism. However, your child may benefit from minor alterations to certain activities or assignments that specifically require speaking.

For example, Elizabeth always took her turn during show-and-tell time, although she relied on nonverbal gestures. When her classmates asked her questions about the object she was showing, the teacher would reword them so that she could answer them by responding "yes" or "no." In that way, Elizabeth was able to nod or shake her head to answer her classmates. Anthony's second-grade teacher would occasionally call on him during class but would ask him to whisper his answer to his friend Max. This classmate would then share Anthony's answer with the rest of the class. During group assignments, Anthony was required to contribute equally. But when the group presented to the class, Anthony participated nonverbally by holding up materials and using nonverbal gestures. Of course, as you've read throughout this book, your child should be expected to participate fully in a nonverbal fashion at school. However, changes to assignments and tasks that require speaking may reduce anxiety for your child and increase her general confidence in the classroom.

It's important for both you and school staff members to view adjustments to oral activities or assignments as a short-term strategy to ensure your child experiences success at school. Alterations of this kind help reduce speaking pressures in the short term, when your child is not yet ready to meet those demands. However, as she progresses up her conversational ladder, more-challenging speaking-related expectations during classroom activities and assignments can be set. For example, next year, in third grade, all of the students in Anthony's class will be required to give a brief speech on a topic of their choice. Although Anthony may not be ready to speak in front of the entire class when that time comes, his teacher may ask him to present his speech to a small number of classmates of his choosing. Max will likely be one member of his chosen audience.

Evaluating Your Child's Academic Progress

In addition to occasional modifications to classroom activities and assignments, you'll need to be aware of the challenges of evaluating your child. Given your child's reluctance to speak within the classroom setting, it can be incredibly difficult for teachers to assess her academic progress. This is often a major concern for teachers, particularly when they need to evaluate oral communication skills, reading skill development, or the acquisition of a second language. Depending on your child's grade level, her teacher may be required to assess various academic skills that are typically demonstrated through oral language. Teachers tend to assess a child's ability to orally communicate ideas during class discussion, her ability to get along with others through observations of verbal interaction, and her early-reading skills by asking her to read aloud. So if your child doesn't speak at all at school, or speaks only infrequently, the teacher cannot easily assess her current abilities. As a result, modifications will need to be made to the standard methods of evaluation.

With some creativity, you and your management team can develop alternative methods for assessing your child's academic progress. Although the unique needs of your child and the requirements for her grade level will dictate the best options, below are some suggested approaches to evaluating the child with selective mutism.

NONVERBAL EVALUATION METHODS

This is probably the most obvious alternative to assessment methods that require speaking. Where possible, the teacher can modify oral evaluation measures in ways that allow for nonverbal responses. For example, your child may be willing to point to pictures to demonstrate her knowledge of word meanings. Or, if your child is old enough to reliably communicate through written methods, oral evaluation might also be translated into a written language task.

USE OF PARENT REPORTS

If an informal gauge of academic progress would be helpful to the teacher, you can often provide information about your child's skill level. For example, if your child's teacher is interested in assessing general reading skills, he or she could provide you with a particular passage or book that your child should read. At home, where your child is most comfortable speaking, you could then ask your child to read the assigned text aloud. With some direction from the teacher in advance regarding the information needed, you could carefully record any errors your child made in decoding, note how persistent she was when sounding out words, and keep track of how long it took her to read the materials.

AUDIOTAPING OR VIDEOTAPING YOUR CHILD

Teachers have often reported that it's quite helpful to have access to a live recording of a child speaking, perhaps during dinner conversation, while singing a favorite song, or while reciting the alphabet. Given how quiet your child may be within the school setting, school staff members often appreciate having the chance to simply hear your child's voice.

More formal samples of audio- or videotaped speaking can also be an invaluable alternative to academic assignments that typically require speaking in the classroom. For example, if your child is expected to give a speech or present an oral book report, perhaps the assignment could be recorded at home instead. Depending on your child's comfort level at the time of evaluation, the teacher might listen to the tape alone, with your child, or with an audience of classmates.

Note, however, that in our experience children's receptivity to being taped can vary significantly from one child to the next. For example, Elizabeth was actually excited to play a tape of herself singing a song she had learned at school for her class. Anthony, on the other hand, was uncomfortable with the idea of others hearing his voice, taped or otherwise. To help your child become comfortable with this short-term alternative to speaking in front of others, give her practice; instead of only recording your child when an assignment is due or the teacher needs to sample her abilities, try taping just for fun. We know of some families who let the tape recorder record their dinnertime conversation and then listen to the tape together afterward. It often makes the child laugh to also hear a sibling or parent talk on the tape. In other households, both the parent and child are recorded during reading at bedtime each night. Given that many children with selective mutism need extra time to be comfortable with new experiences, give your child practice being taped if you can. If she is willing to practice, she'll likely be more relaxed (and more able to show her true abilities) when taping is done for evaluation purposes.

WRITTEN TESTING IN CLASS

For older children with selective mutism, it might also be important to consider modifications to written evaluations. Because children with selective mutism are sometimes more anxious in general, your older child may benefit from having extra time to complete written tests. This might offset her general inhibition or loss of concentration due to anxiety. Similarly, as an alternative to completing tests in the large-group setting of the classroom, your child may benefit from the opportunity to take tests in a separate room where she feels more at ease.

Formalizing Changes to Your Child's Academic Program

Depending on your child's grade level, school, and the school board that governs it, there will be policies that determine how modifications to academic programs are made. Whereas some schools and school boards may be open to informally adjusting your child's program as needed, other school systems may require that your child be formally identified as a student with special learning needs. In keeping with this formal identification of her needs, any modifications to her academic program also become formalized in writing. In North America, this written document is typically called either an *Individual Education Plan* or an *Individualized Education Program* (IEP). It's essentially a written outline of how your child's teacher(s) will modify expectations or instruction to meet your child's needs. Your child's IEP may simply state general accommodations that will be made in order to decrease her anxiety at school, minor modifications to in-class activities, and alternative forms of evaluation where oral participation is typically required. When a plan of this type is formalized, you can expect that school staff will review the appropriateness of the plan on a regular basis (for example, once a year).

Regardless of the country where you live, your child's educational rights and needs are protected by legislation. In the United States, Section 504 and the Individuals with Disabilities Education Act (IDEA) are examples of legislation that protect the rights of students with selective mutism. In Canada, provincial legislation such as the Education Act serves the same purpose—a means to recognize and protect the rights of students with particular learning needs. As a parent, you might find it helpful to find out more about the legislation that guides your child's own school and school board in their commitment to meeting your child's academic needs. You may be able to access this information from your local school board, or you can research this topic on the Internet.

Ensuring your child's academic success and progress in overcoming selective mutism requires careful monitoring and planning. Maintaining momentum as your child works up her conversational ladder is also critical. It's important to anticipate and problem solve around any obstacles that can affect your child's progress. In the next chapter, we'll take a closer look at a range of factors that may contribute to your child's progress and, ultimately, to the rate at which she can overcome selective mutism.

11

Factors That Influence Progress: Revisiting the Case of Peter

CHAPTER OBJECTIVES

In this chapter you will learn about the following:

★ Factors that can influence your child's progress at overcoming selective mutism

★ Challenges you may face while supporting an older child with selective mutism

In the introduction of this book, we gave you two examples of children with selective mutism, Sarah and Peter. A sociable six-year-old girl, Sarah had a fear of speaking that seemed to be specific to the school setting. Sarah was able to speak with ease to her family, other adults in the community, and even a classmate at school in certain situations. She was liked by her peers and enjoyed playing with others, even if she tended to rely on nonverbal communication. We'd hope that, with the use of the strategies described in this book, Sarah would make significant progress in overcoming her selective mutism.

Peter was an eleven-year-old student attending a large inner-city school. Peter's selective mutism and general anxiety in social situations were more extensive. Apart from his immediate family, Peter didn't talk to same-aged peers or adults in the community. He tended to be socially isolated, didn't participate in any extracurricular activities, and preferred to spend time alone. That meant Peter also had fewer opportunities to practice comfortable interaction (both nonverbal and verbal) with others. Given what you know of Peter, what kind of progress do you think he might make in overcoming selective mutism? How do you think his rate of progress might compare to that of Sarah?

FACTORS INFLUENCING PROGRESS

Although we believe that many of the strategies in the book would be helpful for Peter, we also anticipate that his progress would be slower. Do you have any ideas about why that might be? Just as selective mutism appears to be the result of several contributing factors, it's likely that certain factors affect the rate at which a child can overcome it. To date, no research studies have carefully tracked the progress of children with selective mutism and reliably identified factors that influence progress. In our clinical experience, we've found that certain factors, discussed in the pages that follow, can have an impact on how quickly a child can overcome his selective mutism.

Shy or Anxious Temperament

When we first described the factors that seem to contribute to selective mutism (in chapter 2), we talked about a shy or anxious temperament. Children who are shy or slow to warm up to unfamiliar people or circumstances often find it difficult to adjust to first school experiences. They may start to associate anxiety with perceived expectations to perform, speak, or interact with unfamiliar people. The impact of temperament on progress may be a matter of degree. Whereas Sarah might have been described as having a more shy or anxious temperament than some of her classmates, Peter's cautious style is even more extreme. In general, the more extreme a child's shy or anxious temperament, the more time he'll probably need to warm up to new situations. This will be especially applicable in situations that are designed to help him practice speaking comfortably, such as playdates or conversational visits at the school. Ultimately, the extra time needed to become comfortable with new experiences may contribute to slower progress.

Duration of the Mutism

Throughout this book, we've emphasized the importance of early intervention: The sooner your child is helped to work through his fear of speaking, the better. Peter's selective mutism persisted for several years of schooling, which means that the anxiety he experienced when faced with certain speaking situations had also persisted for several years. Essentially, his fear of speaking was reinforced repeatedly through a pattern of avoidance and anxiety-provoking situations that he didn't know how to manage. In general, you can expect that if selective mutism has persisted for several years, it will take much longer for your child to overcome it.

Severity of the Mutism

The extent of the fear of speaking can vary a great deal from one child to another. Some children, like Sarah, seem to experience anxiety when talking specifically in the school context but feel okay in other settings. For Peter, however, his anxiety related to speaking existed in a much broader range of situations. In fact, Peter seemed to be uncomfortable speaking in most situations or settings outside of the family home. Peter's challenge was greater than Sarah's, since he needed to develop a level of comfort with speaking to peers and adults, both inside and outside of the school setting. A child like Peter will probably need more time to overcome his mutism.

Poor Peer Connections Between Home and School

Among the factors described in chapter 2 as possible contributors to selective mutism, we identified an inconsistency in peer relations across settings. Essentially, this occurs when the peers your child might speak with at school, and those your child knows or speaks with in your neighborhood, don't overlap. Sarah, despite being a sociable girl, had not gotten to know classmates who lived in her new neighborhood, since her family moved frequently. Peter's tendency to avoid interactions with others (and his family's preference to spend time within the immediate family) reduced opportunities for him to become more comfortable interacting with anyone outside of the family. Although we might hope that Sarah would be able to make friends with other children in her neighborhood, Peter might find this far more challenging given his social anxiety and avoidance of natural opportunities to become comfortable speaking with others. To overcome his mutism, Peter would need many opportunities to practice socializing with both peers and adults. Peter would need the help, encouragement, and patient support of his parents and the management team.

Maintaining Momentum

Although we talked about momentum at length in chapter 10, we want to emphasize the importance of this concept as a factor that influences your child's progress. Once your child starts overcoming his mutism, it's important to keep him moving up his conversational ladder. Without a doubt, you'll find that it's much more difficult for your child to start making new steps toward speaking with confidence after he's coasted or stopped making progress for a period of time. It'll be much easier for your child (and for those supporting him) to see continued gains if a consistent pace of progress is maintained.

Age and Developmental Level

In general, older children with selective mutism require more time and more intensive support to work through their difficulties. In addition to the fact that the mutism has persisted longer, your child's cognitive maturity will inevitably lead to new challenges. As your child matures, he will become more aware of his difficulties and how they set him apart from others. He may become more self-conscious and more reluctant to participate in anxiety-provoking situations. He may also, either consciously or unconsciously, start to use more sophisticated avoidance strategies. For example, Peter learned that he would never have to tell a stranger the time if he didn't wear a watch! Older children with selective mutism may also physically avoid a wide range of social situations that might cause anxiety.

As your child develops more independence, it becomes more difficult to arrange opportunities for him to practice speaking. He may resist participation in extracurricular activities designed to give him practice interacting with others, and he will probably not be keen on you coming to the school for conversational visits or arranging his social calendar. With older children with selective mutism, your role as a parent support must match your child's developmental level. Given his increased level of maturity, it's often critical to invite him to take on some responsibility for the actual intervention program. Your preteen or teenager might even benefit from becoming an active member of the management team.

We find the general principles underlying the strategies described in this book to be helpful even with an older child with selective mutism. However, you'll need to make modifications to the way they are used. For example, rather than acting as a conversational partner with your child at the school, perhaps you can take on that role at a hockey game in the community or at a school fund-raising function.

Typically, as children grow toward adolescence, it's also important to make peer relations even more of a primary focus. Your child should be encouraged to participate in social activities, regardless of his current level of comfort when speaking with others. Structured extracurricular activities like sports teams or school clubs are often good places for an older child with selective mutism to interact with same-aged peers. As we've described elsewhere in this book, having relationships with classmates will greatly facilitate your child's ability to overcome selective mutism. Your child will likely first become comfortable interacting nonverbally and then later begin to speak with a peer in select settings. Once your child is speaking to at least one peer at the school, the management team can arrange for opportunities for the two students to spend time together. For example, a management team might pair students together for assignments or other school-based activities.

In responding to the needs of an older child with selective mutism, you might also choose to revisit the idea of individual therapy. In chapter 3, you learned about cognitive behavioral therapy, a treatment that is highly effective in treating forms of anxiety. Although CBT is often difficult to use with young children, your older child's level of cognitive maturity may make him a more suitable candidate for this approach. As a complement to social interactions, CBT might help him learn to reduce anxiety by changing his thinking patterns. Even children who are initially uncomfortable speaking to a therapist can often communicate their thoughts through other means, including writing and audio- or videotaping.

Most important, when supporting an older child with selective mutism, it's essential to identify the child's own sources of motivation. Regardless of the number of years that it has persisted, children often have a strong desire to overcome their mutism. Exploring your child's own personal goals for working through his difficulty can ensure his progress and ultimately his success in overcoming the fear of speaking.

12

Preparing Your Child for School Transitions and Looking Ahead to Next Year

CHAPTER OBJECTIVES

In this chapter you will learn about the following:

★ The benefits of preparing your child for transitions at school

★ How to talk your child through an experience in advance to prepare her

★ How to help your child practice in advance for a new experience

★ Strategies you can use over the summer months to maintain your child's comfort level and current step on the conversational ladder

★ Tasks you can undertake in the current school year to plan for your child's success next year

As you've read elsewhere in this book (and probably already know from your own experience), many children with selective mutism have things in common with other anxious children. In particular, children with selective mutism often have difficulty adapting to transitions or changes in daily routines. As your child gradually works to overcome her selective mutism, there'll be times when she is faced with changes in school routines that could disrupt her general comfort levels and her overall progress. Sometimes these will be unexpected changes, such as the absence of a friend or teacher due to an illness. Other times the transitions will be expected, such as scheduled school vacations.

As the parent of a child who has difficulty adjusting to changes, you might find it helpful to think about ways you can make transition times more comfortable for your child. The sooner your child settles in to her new routine, the sooner she'll be ready to take further steps up her conversational ladder.

Several good books describe strategies that parents can use to help their child manage anxious times or adjust to new experiences, including *Keys to Parenting Your Anxious Child* (Manassis 1996) and *Helping Your Anxious Child* (Rapee et al. 2000). To help your child prepare for transitions that can be anticipated, there are two main strategies that we recommend: discussing the transition in advance and providing opportunities for exposure ahead of time

DISCUSS ANXIETY-PROVOKING TRANSITIONS IN ADVANCE

If you know that your child's classroom teacher will be taking a leave of absence or that a favorite classmate will be away from school next week, discuss this with your child in advance. Outline what will happen and help her develop new expectations for the experience. For example, six-year-old Jackie was much more at ease with a substitute bus driver when her mother discussed the situation with her the weekend before. Jackie and her mother talked about where she'd sit on the bus that week and whom she'd like to sit beside. Jackie even decided that she might wave good-bye at the end of the day to the new bus driver, just like she did with her regular bus driver.

Similarly, Eric, a ten-year-old who hated to miss school, benefited from a chance to talk about what it would be like to return to school after his illness the previous week. His parents reminded him of what his schedule would look like the first day back, how he'd find out what lessons he'd missed, and when he might get a chance to catch up with his best friend.

In general, these kinds of previewing discussions can help to ease your child's anxieties by giving information about what can be expected. With this type of preparation, she sees the new experience as more predictable and tends to feel more in control. Of course, you'll need to use your own judgment in deciding how much discussion is needed and how far in advance the discussion should take place. For some children, the more information and time to prepare, the better. For other anxious children, too much discussion too far in advance can actually increase anxiety in anticipation of the event. Think about what you know about other transitions your child has successfully made. What approach do you think would work best with your own child?

PROVIDE PRACTICE EXPERIENCES IN ADVANCE

When you can anticipate a change or new experience for your child, it can often be helpful to provide her with the opportunity to test out the situation in advance. For example, Jackie's parents took her to visit the dance studio a week before her first class started. And Eric's father made sure he and his son played a couple of games on the soccer field before the first practice of the season. Can you think of situations in which your child might benefit from a chance to explore a new experience in advance? By introducing her to an unfamiliar (and potentially anxiety-provoking) situation beforehand, the unknown, which often triggers anxiety, becomes more familiar and comfortable. When your child needs to enter that situation for real, she'll know what to expect and likely be able to approach it with more confidence and make the transition more smoothly.

PREPARING YOUR CHILD TO RETURN TO SCHOOL AFTER A BREAK

Scheduled school vacations over the holiday season, spring break, or the summer months are important transition times for your child, and they require special consideration. Because they can affect your child's progress in overcoming selective mutism, it's important for you and your child's management team to plan for these breaks accordingly.

During times when your child is away from the school environment, you'll need to think of other ways to maintain her comfort level with school and her general progress in overcoming selective mutism. The same strategies described for supporting your child through small transitions can also be applied to longer-term breaks in school routines.

Maintaining Your Child's Comfort Level at School

In anticipation of your child's return to school following a holiday break, you can discuss the transition in advance. This is often a particularly useful strategy following the summer break and your child's transition to a new grade. You might talk with your child about what she expects will happen on the first day back, the children she thinks might be in her class, and what subjects she's looking forward to studying. Informal discussion and planning about the coming school year can serve to decrease any anticipatory anxiety your child might be experiencing.

Similarly, by providing your child with exposure opportunities before a return to school, you will help her to become more comfortable with the transition. In essence, you'll be giving her a head start in warming up to this new experience. There are many creative ways you can provide your child with this warm-up time in the school setting. For example, Eric's parents made sure their son had lots of opportunities to practice his soccer (and his confident speaking!) on the school playground over the summer months. Sometimes, a playmate from his class also came along for some fun and they even peeked through a window into their new classroom and played a game of I Spy. Jackie's mother took photos of Jackie, her friends, the next year's teacher, and the school itself at the end of her kindergarten year. With the help of her mother, Jackie then made a photo album and added her own drawings of her favorite times at school. During the summer months, Jackie periodically took the album out to show it to a relative or to talk about the upcoming school year with her parents.

As another important way to ensure she'd be comfortable starting school again in the fall and speaking in that setting, Jackie's parents arranged a school tour at the end of summer. Jackie brought her younger sister along to proudly show where her new classroom would be and talk about where she'd spend most of her time during the school day. Jackie was even able to visit her new classroom and meet her new teacher. On a second trip to the school before the fall term started, Jackie returned with a classmate and good friend, Katie. Do you think summer visits to the school could help your child make the adjustment to a new academic year and provide her with some practice speaking at school before classes begin?

Maintaining Your Child's Step on the Conversational Ladder

During times when your child is not attending school, it's also important to think about ways to maintain your child's level of comfort when speaking in school-related situations. When the school itself is closed to your child during a holiday break, can you think of other ways that you could arrange conversational practice for your child?

When your child is away from school for an extended period of time, we strongly recommend that you arrange frequent playdates with a preferred classmate. This might be a challenge to arrange during the busy winter holiday season, but it might be easier to do during the spring break and certainly over the summer months. As your child continues to get practice interacting with classmates, think about ways you can keep the school experience alive for her. Jackie's mother, for example, set up the living room like a classroom and encouraged Jackie and her friend Katie to play school. In addition to taking him to regular soccer games on the school grounds, Eric's parents encouraged him to write a letter to his new teacher describing all of his favorite summer adventures. Can you think of ways that your child can continue to think about and remain comfortable with school during class breaks?

Looking Ahead to the Next School Year

Although your child may not be making a transition to a new grade and teacher anytime soon, you'll find it helpful to know what you can do when you get there. Ideally, in late spring, the management team should begin making plans for the coming school year. Some of the issues that should be discussed include the following:

- **Changes to the membership of the management team.** If possible, determine what members of the current management team will be available to be part of next year's team. The new classroom teacher will be an important addition to the team and should be invited to an end-of-the-year meeting. This will give the new teacher a chance to do some preliminary learning about selective mutism, the ways the management team assists your child, and any modifications to your child's academic program that may be required.

- **Initial scheduling of next fall's first management team meeting.** Discuss when and where the management team will meet in early fall to plan for the new school year.

- **Your child's class assignment for the coming year.** Depending on the size of your child's school, there may be more than one class she could be assigned to next year. If there's some flexibility in the decision of class assignment, the management team should think about the peers who will be assigned to each class and the teacher involved. For example, if one of next year's teachers has previously taught your child, the management team may want to consider whether your child would benefit from continuing this familiar relationship or establishing one with someone new. It's most important to consider a class assignment that allows your child to be in the company of preferred peers and classmates whom she speaks to either in or outside of school.

■ **Access to the school building over the summer.** Typically, in the weeks before the new school year begins, staff members may be in the building making preparations. Often that's a good time to arrange a school visit with your child. Before the summer break begins, make sure you know whom to contact and when to arrange the school visit.

When it's time to start planning for your child's next school year, you can come back to this section of the book to remind yourself of what you can do. We hope the following task list will serve as a useful reminder as you ensure your child's continued progress and success in the school year ahead.

Because it is a relatively rare condition, selective mutism is not well understood by the public, many educators, and other professionals committed to the well-being of our children. Few resources are available to provide current information on the condition and how we can best help children affected by it. For you, the parent faced with this perplexing disorder and the many questions that it brings up, we hope that this book has provided some answers. Most important, through reading this book, we hope that you have developed an understanding of the condition, how to use the intervention strategies described, and your significant role in helping your child overcome selective mutism.

	Task list: Preparing for the summer transition and the new school year	
✓	**Task**	**Description**
	Friends	List friends from next year's class whom your child can play with over the summer.
	Activities	List activities and places that encourage your child to speak and play comfortably with friends.
	Playdates with friends	Plan frequent get-togethers for your child and her classmates.
	Class visits	Consider making a trip to your child's new classroom before school starts. Invite along people your child will speak to during the year. (Longer visits are often more helpful.)
	Class selection	With the management team, decide which class best meets your child's needs.
	Peer selection	List peers with whom your child currently speaks or plays. Ensure that these students are in the same class, if possible.
	Management team	Identify members of your fall management team.
	Teacher introduction	Introduce next year's teacher to the team and provide information regarding selective mutism. Develop a fall plan.
	Fall seating	Consider ideal seating arrangements for your child.
	Fall seat mates	Identify students your child could sit beside.
	Fall team meeting	Schedule your first fall management team meeting.

References

American Psychiatric Association. 1994. *Diagnostic and statistical manual of mental disorders* (4ᵗʰ ed). Washington, DC: Author.

Beidel, D. C., Turner, S. M., & Morris, T. L. 1999. Psychopathology of childhood social phobia. *Journal of the American Academy of Child and Adolescent Psychiatry, 38*, 643-650.

Bergman, R. L., Piacentini, J., & McCracken, J. T. 2002. Prevalence and description of selective mutism in a school-based sample. *Journal of the American Academy of Child and Adolescent Psychiatry, 41*, 938-946.

Black, B., & Uhde, T. W. 1995. Psychiatric characteristics of children with selective mutism: A pilot study. *Journal of the American Academy of Child and Adolescent Psychiatry, 34*(7), 847-856.

Boivin, M., Hymel, S., & Bukowski, W. M. 1995. The roles of social withdrawal, peer rejection, and victimization by peers in predicting loneliness and depressed mood in children. *Development and Psychopathology, 7*, 765-786.

Cunningham, C. E. (2001, Summer). *COPEing with selective mutism: A collaborative school-based approach. Consultant's manual.* (Available from McMaster Children's Hospital, Chedoke Child and Family Centre, Attention Randi Knight, P.O. Box 2000, Hamilton, ON, Canada, L8N 3Z5. See the Web site at http://www.psychdirect.com/children/selectivemutism.htm for a downloadable order form.)

Cunningham, C. E., Cataldo, M. F., Mallion, C., & Keyes, J. B. 1984. A review and controlled single case evaluation of behavioral approaches to the management of elective mutism. *Child and Family Behavior Therapy*, 5(4), 25-49.

Cunningham, C. E., McHolm, A., Boyle, M. H., & Patel, S. 2004. Behavioral and emotional adjustment, family functioning, academic performance, and social relationships in children with selective mutism. *Journal of Child Psychology and Psychiatry*, 45(8), 1363-1372.

Dummit, E. S., Klein, R. G., Tancer, N. K., Asche, B., & Martin, J. 1996. Fluoxetine treatment of children with selective mutism: An open trial. *Journal of the American Academy of Child and Adolescent Psychiatry*, 35(5), 615-621.

Dummit, E. S., Klein, R. G., Tancer, N. K., Asche, B., Martin, J., & Fairbanks, J. A. 1997. Systematic assessment of 50 children with selective mutism. *Journal of the American Academy of Child and Adolescent Psychiatry*, 36, 653-660.

Elizur, Y., & Perednik, R. 2003. Prevalence and description of selective mutism in immigrant and native families: A controlled study. *Journal of the American Academy of Child and Adolescent Psychiatry*, 42(12), 1451-1459.

Hayden, T. L. 1980. The classification of elective mutism. *Journal of the American Academy of Child and Adolescent Psychiatry*, 19, 118-133.

Hofmann, S. G., Moscovitch, D. A., & Heinrichs, N. 2003. Evolutionary mechanisms of fear and anxiety. *Journal of Cognitive Psychotherapy*, 16(3), 317-330.

Johnson, M., & Wintgens, A. 2001. *The selective mutism resource manual*. Bicester, Oxford: Speechmark Publishing Ltd.

Kendall, P. C., Chu, B. C., Pimentel, S. S., & Choudhury, M. 2000. Treating anxiety disorders in youth. In P. C. Kendall (Ed.), *Child and Adolescent Therapy: Cognitive-behavioral procedures* (pp. 235-287). New York: Guilford.

Kristensen, H. 2000. Selective mutism and comorbidity with developmental disorder/delay, anxiety disorder, and elimination disorder. *Journal of the American Academy of Child and Adolescent Psychiatry*, 39, 249-256.

Kristensen, H. 2001. Multiple informants' report of emotional and behavioural problems in a nation-wide sample of selective mute children and controls. *European Journal of Child and Adolescent Psychiatry, 10,* 135-142.

Kristensen, H., & Torgensen, S. 2001. MCMI-II personality traits and symptom traits in parents of children with selective mutism: A case-control study. *Journal of Abnormal Psychology, 110,* 648-652.

Kumpulainen, K., Rasanen, E., Raaska, H., & Somppi, V. 1998. Selective mutism among second-graders in elementary school. *European Journal of Child and Adolescent Psychiatry, 7,* 24-29.

Manassis, K. 1996. *Keys to parenting your anxious child.* Hauppauge, New York: Barron's Educational Series, Inc.

Ollendick, T. H., King, N. J., & Muris, P. 2002. Fears and phobias in children: Phenomenology, epidemiology, and aetiology. *Child and Adolescent Mental Health, 7*(3), 98-106.

Pellegrini, A. D., Bartini, M., & Brooks, F. 2001. School bullies, victims, and aggressive victims: Factors relating to group affiliation and victimization in early adolescence. *Journal of Educational Psychology, 91,* 216-224.

Pionek Stone, B., Kratochwill, T. R., Sladezcek, I., & Serlin, R. C. 2002. Treatment of selective mutism: A best-evidence synthesis. *School Psychology Quarterly, 17*(2), 168-190.

Rapee, R., Spence, S., Cobham, V., & Wignall, A. 2000. *Helping your anxious child.* Oakland, Calif.: New Harbinger Publications.

Remschmidt, H., Poller, M., Herpertz-Dahlmann, B., Henninghausen, K., & Gutenbrunner, C. 2001. A follow-up study of 45 patients with elective mutism. *European Archives of Psychiatry and Clinical Neuroscience, 251*(6), 284-296.

Steinhausen, H., & Juzi, C. 1996. Elective mutism: An analysis of 100 cases. *Journal of the American Academy of Child and Adolescent Psychiatry, 35,* 606-614.

Vecchio, J. L., & Kearney, C. A. 2005. Selective mutism in children: Comparison to youths with and without anxiety disorders. *Journal of Psychopathology and Behavioral Assessment, 27*(1), 31-37.

Angela E. McHolm, Ph.D., is director of the Selective Mutism Service at McMaster Children's Hospital in Hamilton, ON, Canada. The Selective Mutism Service offers consultation and intervention services to children, their families, and professionals such as school personnel, speech and language pathologists, and mental health clinicians who support children with selective mutism. She is assistant professor in the Department of Psychiatry and Behavioural Neurosciences in the Faculty of Health Sciences at McMaster University in Hamilton, ON, Canada. McHolm also holds an associate faculty appointment in the Department of Psychology at the University of Guelph, where she trains students and provides psychological services to local children and their families.

Charles E. Cunningham, Ph.D., is a staff psychologist at McMaster Children's Hospital and professor in the Department of Psychiatry and Behavioural Neurosciences in the Faculty of Health Sciences at McMaster University—both in Hamilton, ON, Canada. He also holds the Jack Laidlaw Chair in Patient-Centered Health Care at McMaster University. He has published and presented widely on various topics related to children's mental health. Within the field of selective mutism, he has approximately thirty years' clinical experience and has coauthored various manuscripts including a review of effective behavioral approaches to the treatment of selective mutism.

Melanie K. Vanier, MA, at the time of writing this book, was staff clinician with the Selective Mutism Service at McMaster Children's Hospital in Hamilton, ON, Canada. In her direct clinical work with children with and their families, she has collaborated on the development and writing of a manual for a group workshop series offered to parents and professionals who work with selective mutism.

Foreword writer Ronald M. Rapee, Ph.D., is professor of psychology at MacQuarrie University in Sydney, Australia. He is author of **Helping Your Anxious Child** and **Treating Anxious Children and Adolescents**.

Some Other
New Harbinger Titles

Helping A Child with Nonverbal Learning Disorder, 2nd edition
Item 5266 $15.95

The Introvert & Extrovert in Love, Item 4863 $14.95

Helping Your Socially Vulnerable Child, Item 4580 $15.95

Life Planning for Adults with Developmental Disabilities, Item 4511 $19.95

But I Didn't Mean That! Item 4887 $14.95

The Family Intervention Guide to Mental Illness, Item 5068 $17.95

It's So Hard to Love You, Item 4962 $14.95

The Turbulent Twenties, Item 4216 $14.95

The Balanced Mom, Item 4534 $14.95

Helping Your Child Overcome Separation Anxiety & School Refusal,
Item 4313 $14.95

When Your Child Is Cutting, Item 4375 $15.95

Helping Your Child with Selective Mutism, Item 416X $14.95

Sun Protection for Life, Item 4194 $11.95

Helping Your Child with Autism Spectrum Disorder, Item 3848 $17.95

Teach Me to Say It Right, Item 4038 $13.95

Grieving Mindfully, Item 4011 $14.95

The Courage to Trust, Item 3805 $14.95

The Gift of ADHD, Item 3899 $14.95

The Power of Two Workbook, Item 3341 $19.95

Adult Children of Divorce, Item 3368 $14.95

*Fifty Great Tips, Tricks, and Techniques to Connect
with Your Teen*, Item 3597 $10.95

Helping Your Child with OCD, Item 3325 $19.95

Helping Your Depressed Child, Item 3228 $14.95

Call **toll free, 1-800-748-6273,** or log on to our online bookstore at **www.newharbinger.com** to order. Have your Visa or Mastercard number ready. Or send a check for the titles you want to New Harbinger Publications, Inc., 5674 Shattuck Ave., Oakland, CA 94609. Include $4.50 for the first book and 75¢ for each additional book, to cover shipping and handling. (California residents please include appropriate sales tax.) Allow two to five weeks for delivery.

Prices subject to change without notice.